'*Work with Me* is the perfect blend of Annis' cutting-edge research and insights into the minds of men and women at work, and Gray's enduring contribution to our understanding of male-female personal relations. Together, Annis and Gray provide the perfect relational guide for men and women looking for happiness and success through greater understanding as colleagues, partners, and parents'

Jack Canfield, author and co-creator of the
'Chicken Soup for the Soul' series

'What a concept! Men being men and women being women. It's about time we put to rest the failed notion that we are all the same. Annis and Gray introduce an entirely new way to think and talk about gender equality in the 21st century. *Work with Me* is a perfect blend of work-life and personal-life messages. No other book tackles the issue of men and women working and winning together'

Raymond Aaron, *New York Times* bestselling author of
Double Your Income Doing What You Love

'Annis and Gray bravely reveal the blind spots that perpetually prevent men and women from understanding and appreciating their gender differences, not hiding or suppressing their authentic natures, and as a result, finding greater success and happiness in their professional and personal lives'

Dr. Fabrizio Mancini, bestselling author of *The Power of Self-Healing*

'*Work with Me* is a landmark work that examines today's workplace opportunities and challenges through both an economic and social interaction lens and demonstrates why gender intelligence – not gender equality – will inspire a culture of inclusiveness and create a sustainable source of economic advantage for, individuals, leaders, and their organizations'

Lara Warner, Chief Financial Officer, Credit Suisse Investment Bank

'No doubt about it. Group intelligence is highest when both genders problem solve together. Now Barbara Annis and John Gray show us how to get the job done! If this book doesn't make you think, you are brain dead!'

Dr. Wendy Walsh, Human Behavior Expert, CNN and
The O'Reilly Factor

'It's time to get smart about Gender Intelligence. If anyone on Earth – or Venus or Mars – can sort out these complex relationships, John Gray and Barbara Annis can. "Work" your way through this remarkable book!'

Harvey Mackay, #1 *New York Times* bestselling author of
Swim With The Sharks Without Being Eaten Alive

'It seems that most books written on gender relations implores women to act more like men and deplores men for acting like themselves. Men and women want to find ways to work and succeed together, and to do so by being their authentic selves. *Work with Me* shows us how, with equal learning for women and men. It is refreshingly non-judgemental – neither gender is to be blamed or "fixed". Annis and Gray reveal that gender differences are not weaknesses but strengths that are often misunderstood and undervalued by both genders. *Work with Me* is an enjoyable and enlightening read, filled with practical information supported by empirical data, scientific explanations, and dozens of anecdotes that skilfully and warmly reflect gender interactions in our professional and personal lives'

Valerie Sorbie, Chief Administrative Officer, BMO Capital Markets

'Annis and Gray confront, head on, the elephant in the room. Men and women are not the same, are quite different, and actually complement each other perfectly. It's about time we begin to understand, appreciate, and value each other's ways of thinking and acting. *Work with Me* bravely illuminates the path to greater understanding'

Jane Allen, Chief Diversity Officer, Deloitte Canada

WORK WITH ME

BARBARA ANNIS
& JOHN GRAY

piatkus

PIATKUS

First published in the US in 2013 by Palgrave Macmillan,
a division of St. Martin's Press LLC, New York
First published in Great Britain in 2013 by Piatkus

This paperback edition published in 2016 by Piatkus

13 5 7 9 10 8 6 4 2

A CIP catalogue record for this book
is available from the British Library.

ISBN 978-0-349-40502-5

Design by Letra Libre
Printed and bound in Great Britain by
Clays Ltd, St Ives plc

Papers used by Piatkus are from well-managed forests
and other responsible sources.

MIX
Paper from
responsible sources
FSC® C104740

Piatkus
An imprint of
Little, Brown Book Group
Carmelite House
50 Victoria Embankment
London EC4Y 0DZ

An Hachette UK Company
www.hachette.co.uk

www.piatkus.co.uk

To my husband, Paul Reed Currie, whose amazing support, love, and integrity I always admire and treasure.

And to my wonderful children, Lauren, Sasha, Stéphane, and Christian; my bonus children, Zachary, Kelly, and Jeremy; and my grandchildren, Colin, Cameron, Alaia, Brydan, Jake, Riley, and Grayson.

—Barbara

With love and affection to my wife, Bonnie Gray, and our daughters Lauren, Juliet, and Shannon. Their love has supported me to be the best I can be, and to share with others what we have learned together as a family.

—John

CONTENTS

ACKNOWLEDGMENTS

A SPECIAL THANK YOU TO LEE BROWER, WHO HAD THE VISION TO introduce the idea of bringing two global experts together to combine their insights from both their business and personal lives.

We wish to thank our senior editor, John Fayad, for his dedication and hard work. We also wish to thank the many thousands of men and women who have participated in this work and have ensured that it made a lasting difference in their lives. Thank you to Karen Wolny and the team at Palgrave Macmillan, and our literary agent, Carol Mann, for bringing this work into the world. We also want to acknowledge our friends, colleagues, and clients for having made tremendous contributions in their sphere of influence.

BARBARA ANNIS

I wish to thank Lee Akazaki, Kenchiro Akiyama, Jane Allen, Jennifer Allyn, Shahla Aly, Greg Van Asperen, Beth Axelrod, Robin Baliszewski, Jim Beqaj, Jill Beresford, Gina Bianchini, Lynda Bowles, Stephanie Hanbury Brown, Woody Buckner, James Bush, Susan Cartsonis, Kenneth Chenault, Jennifer Christie, Judy Dahm, Christa Dowling, Nancy Elder, Carol Evans, Dr. Helen Fisher, Nancy Forsyth, Gaby Giglio, Ed Gilligan, Neena Gupta, Dr. Ruben Gur, Bruce Haase, Nadine Hack, Irena Halsey, Jane Hewson, Jan Hill, Arianna Huffington, Swanee Hunt, Dr. Joseph Jaworski, Elisabeth Jensen, Sonya Kunkel,

Dr. George Labovitz, Stan Labovitz, Carolyn Lawrence, Bruce Leamon, Chuck Ledsinger, Dr. Marianne Legato, Maria LeRose, Pernille Spiers-Lopez, Renee Lundholm, Anne Madison, Susanna Margolis, Marguerite McLeod, Ramón Martín, Graciela Meibar, Dr. Keith Merron, Dr. Anne Moir, Betsy Myers, Lisa Olinda, Hubert Saint-Onge, Paola Corna Pellegrini, Kerrie Peraino, Phyllis Stewart Pires, Allison Pogemiller, Alan Richter, Eiko Saito, Nicole Schwab, Maria Shriver, Dr. Janet Smith, Jim Hagerman Snabe, Val Sorbie, Erin Stein, Claudia Studle, Kate Sweetman, Aniela Unguresan, Dr. Karin Verland, Dr. Elena Vigna, Lara Warner, James Ward, Donna Wilson, Marie Wilson, Oprah Winfrey, Dr. Sandra Witelson, Anka Wittenberg, and Janet Wood.

A special thank-you to: John Hart, CEO of the Gender Intelligence Institute and the Impact Center, whose dedication and commitment to advancing Gender Intelligence and Collaborative Leadership ranging from the White House to our powerful emerging leaders;

All the amazing, deeply committed women leaders and staff at the Women's Leadership Board, Harvard Kennedy School; to the Gender Equality Project Geneva, I am honored to partner with you in creating a world where men and women are equally valued and respected in all aspects of economic, political, and social life; to the remarkable board members of the Institute for Women's Studies in the Arab World (IWSAW) at the Lebanese American University in Beirut, Lebanon, for their enduring contribution to empowering women in the Arab world through development, programs and education; and to all the organizations and their men and women embracing Gender Intelligence for the want of working and succeeding together including American Express, Bentley University, Blake, Cassels & Graydon, BMO Financial Group, Choice Hotels International, CIBC, Costco, Crayola, Credit Suisse, Danish CEO Network, Deloitte, the Department of Justice, the Department of National Defense, Deutsche Bank, Disney, Dove–Unilever, eBay, EDS, Electrolux, Federal Business Development Bank, Financial Times, Ford Motor Company, Fordham University, Goldman Sachs,

Goodman & Carr, Greenberg Traurig, Harvard University, HSBC Bank, IBM, IKEA, Imperial Oil, Industry Canada, Kellogg's, Kvinfo, Johnson & Johnson, Lever Ponds, Levi Strauss, Mattel, McDonalds, Microsoft, Molson, Motorola, National Defense Canada, Nissan, Novartis, Oliver Wyman, Pax World, Pearson Education, Pfizer, Prentice Hall, PricewaterhouseCoopers, RBC Financial, RBC Investment Group, SAP, Scotia Bank, SMBC, Sunlife Insurance, Swedish Chamber of Commerce, Symcor, Tambrands, Toshiba, Treasury Board, UBS Investments, Unilever, Wells Fargo Women of Influence, Wood Gundy Securities, Xerox, and Xstrata.

JOHN GRAY

I want to thank my wife, Bonnie Gray, for her continued love and support in our personal relationship as well as in the office, where she continues to update me on how to support the women we work with. I would also like to thank our three daughters and their partners, Shannon and Jon, Juliet and Dan, Lauren and Glade, and our adorable grandchildren Sophia, Bo, Brady, and Makena.

So many thanks go to my team that makes this work happen. My executive assistant, Hallina Popko, Jon Myers, marketing director of MarsVenus.com, Marcy Wynne, director of customer service, Glade Truitt, director of video production for my daily online blog, Jeff Owens, director of AskMarsVenus.com, Rich Bernstein, president and director of MarsVenusCoaching.com and Mars Venus Coaching Training, Amy Kamstra, manager of Mars Venus Coaching Training as well as all the following Mars Venus Executive Coaches around the world: Karen Leckie, Lesley Edwards, Alan Ogden (Canada), Rosa Botran (Guatemala), Jessy Keller (Mexico), Dalal Al Janaie (Kuwait), Kal Sharaf (Jordan), Michele Festa, Caterina Tornani (Italy), Michael Kubina (Germany), Nesan Naidoo (Australia), Niru Kumar (India), Melodie Tucker, Liza Davis, Susan Berke, and Lyndsay Katauskas (USA).

Adapting the Mars Venus Message to meet the challenges of the many diverse companies and organizations listed below has refined and shaped the insights in *Work with Me* to improve communication between men and women in their professional and personal lives. I want to thank: AIG Financial, Allstate Insurance, American Airlines, American Mothers Convention, America Online (AOL), Anthony Robbins Company, ARCA Enterprises, AT&T, BermanBraun, Better Business Bureau, Book Passage, Borders Bookstores, California's Women Conference, Central Intelligence Agency, Charles Schwab, Chopra Center for Wellbeing, the Coca Cola Company, Commonwealth Bank, Coors Brewing Company, Crucial.com, Daimler-Chrysler, Dr. Oz and ZoCo Productions, Emerson University, eWomen Network, EXL, Ford Australia, Ford Motor Company, Governor of Utah Marriage Day, Harvey Mackay Roundtable, IBM, ICMI Speakers Bureau—Australia, Isagenix, Johnson and Johnson, Kmart, Kuwait Oil Company, Lifestyle Medicine Summit, Lucent Technologies, Luxor, McDonald's, Merck Pharmaceuticals, MGM Resorts International, Microsoft, Mortgage and Finance Association of Australia, National Association for Hospice and Home Care, National Broadcasting Company, National Institute of Standards and Measurements, National Public Radio, National Speakers Association, Natural Factors, Nightingale Conant, Nokia, Oprah Winfrey and Harpo Productions, Oracle, Parker Chiropractic Seminars, Pat Vitucci and Associates, Peak Potentials, Preferred Nutrition, Princess Cruise Lines, Public Broadcasting Service, Rotary Club, Sheraton Towers International, Smart Marriages, Society For Human Resource Management, Sony Pictures, Stanford University, Suisse Vitamins, Summit Entertainment, Suzanne Somers, TED, the American Society of Bariatric Physicians, the Boeing Company, the Commonwealth Club, the Pachamama Alliance, the Pollack PR Marketing Group, Toyota Australia, Toys "R" Us, Transformational Leadership Council, U.S. Army, Wal-Mart, Walt Disney Corporation, WPO/YPO, and YourTango.

INTRODUCTION

HAVE YOU EVER FELT THIS WAY, OR HEARD COMMENTS SUCH AS these expressed by friends or coworkers?

"I'm tired of being excluded and having my ideas dismissed."

"Being the best person for the job means nothing here."

"I have to be so careful in what I say and do."

"I can't and won't act like someone I'm not."

Or, maybe these scenarios describe you or someone you know.

Susan graduated at the top of her MBA class and landed a well-paying, entry level position at a major firm. She loves to collaborate. She excels at creating alliances and developing those relationships. You can see that in her expanding client base. They love doing business with her.

Susan is trying, though failing, to fit in with the men at the office. She had no clue that the culture would be so competitive. It wasn't that way at the university. She feels she doesn't stand a chance to be promoted, regardless of her contribution. Tired of being undervalued and excluded, Susan is looking for a company that appreciates her and offers her room to grow.

Bill loves to compete. To him, work is like a daily sporting event and lunch is halftime. He's a good strategic planner and a get-it-done person. He's at his best when he can work and solve problems alone. His performance reviews reflect his achievements. His company truly values Bill's efforts.

But Bill has difficulty working on teams and waiting for decisions. He's no longer sanctioned to work independently and act in ways others now consider "too quick and reckless." At the last staff meeting, he thinks he said something wrong to one of the women executives, but he's not sure what it was he said. He feels he was misunderstood. Bill is faltering—he can feel it but doesn't know how to correct it.

We often hear comments and stories such as these in our workshops and seminars. We know Susan and Bill. They are real people, and they are not alone. There are millions of others just like them who are stuck, or failing, or quitting—not because of their abilities, but because they haven't figured out how to work effectively with the opposite gender.

We all want to work more successfully with each other, but we're unsure how. We don't understand why the women or men we work with communicate, solve problems, make decisions, and deal with stress the way they do. Women and men may see the same things, but they do so through a completely different set of lenses, very often thinking and talking past each other.

The conventional wisdom that women and men are no different from each other, have the same aspirations, and are expected to achieve their goals in the same fashion is precisely why we're experiencing a cultural breakdown today instead of the equality breakthrough we expected by now.

In blind pursuit of gender sameness, we've painted ourselves into a corner. In trying to fix women to act less as themselves and more like men, and in chastising men for behaving as men, we've set in motion a perpetual cycle of miscommunication and misunderstanding. We're not being authentic with each other and even less so with ourselves.

COMING TOGETHER

Epiphanies tend to put us on paths that lead to even greater discoveries and, at times, amazing synergies.

As authors working in similar fields, we were very familiar with each other's work. John Gray's message in his groundbreaking book, *Men Are from Mars, Women Are from Venus,* had global impact. Through stories and examples that people could connect with, he revealed why and how women and men communicate, think, feel, and react differently, which improved thousands of relationships and saved marriages. Similarly, Barbara Annis, in her work on gender intelligence and inclusive leadership, pioneered a transformational shift in cultural attitudes on the importance of gender unity to personal success. Her book, *Same Words, Different Language,* helped career-oriented men and women remove barriers to their professional growth and personal happiness and discover a new level of conversation and collaboration.

Together, we discovered that we were talking to the same individuals but in two different arenas—helping men and women as coworkers, bound by a desire to succeed and find greater understanding and success in their working lives; and helping them as couples, bound by a desire to love, find greater understanding and trust in their personal lives.

What brought us together and why we are speaking together in this book is because these two worlds—our two lives—are not as separate as they were when we first began our respective journeys.

Paralleling men's and women's desire to understand and be understood in the workplace and at home is a growing need to find congruity in their work life and personal life. We're looking for ways to orchestrate our jobs, relationships, and responsibilities so that everyone feels appreciated and fulfilled. But we're often blind to each other's needs and expectations, and often unable to express and satisfy our own needs.

RECOGNIZING OUR BLIND SPOTS

When driving a car, our sides and rearview mirrors don't often reveal everything we need to see. We find we have blind spots and turn our heads lest we miss something. We don't resist the fact that we have blind spots or deny that they exist; we accept their presence and make every effort to improve our vision. We do it to be less of a hazard to others; we do it out of concern for those close to us; we do it to practice self-care.

Quite similar are the obstructions that prevent men and women from seeing the other gender in the clearest and best possible light—what we call "gender blind spots": incorrect assumptions held by both men and women, stereotypic baggage that continues to cause our miscommunications and fuel our misunderstandings.

Men and women truly want to see each other clearly, but they can't read the other gender well enough. They can't communicate cogently. They don't know how to listen or what to listen for. They're trying their best to work together effectively and find greater happiness in their personal lives, but they're coming up short in so many ways.

The purpose of our book is to expose and eliminate our blind spots conclusively. It's time for a cultural shift in our thinking. What we need now—more than ever before—is a new level of awareness and attentiveness to each other's needs, a depth of understanding we call "gender intelligence."

GROWING IN GENDER INTELLIGENCE

So what do we mean by "gender intelligence"? It's an awareness of the intrinsic nature of men and women beyond the physical and cultural. It's an understanding of and appreciation for our differences. It is not assuming we're all alike and tolerating those differences when they appear. Nor is it about modifying our behavior or learning new behaviors that are not authentic to ourselves.

Gender intelligence recognizes that gender is a function of both nature and nurture—first informed by nature, then shaped by society and culture. Only by first understanding the nature of our differences can we then gain the insight into how to nurture, develop, and complement our differences, instead of denying and suppressing our own uniqueness and that of the other gender.

The number-one complaint women have in the workplace is not feeling valued or appreciated, because men often misread women's intentions, misinterpret their actions, and fail to recognize their strengths. It's not that men don't want to understand; they simply don't know how to read women's thoughts and actions. The same holds true for women. They often misread men's intentions and behaviors because they don't understand what compels men to think and act as they do.

We're unsure of how to best work with the women and men in the offices and cubicles alongside ours, or in the conference rooms, or on our teams, or at lunch, or with the person in the corner office. We feel we have to be careful in what we say, and at times we don't even know what to say. Our challenge at work isn't in our ability to do our jobs; it's in our inability to authentically engage with the other gender.

Gender intelligence enables women and men to understand each other's way of thinking and acting. It exposes and eliminates our blind spots. It lifts us to a new level of conversation. And it encourages us to include and work with each other more confidently, more willingly—not by expecting each other to think and behave the same, but rather by finding and valuing the complement in our differences.

Work with Me reveals, for the first time, survey results of over 100,000 quantitative and qualitative statements from men and women, captured through a powerful, custom-designed diagnostic survey that depicts the candid attitudes of women and men at work. This predictive matrix analyzes the open-ended responses of women and men to reveal not only how but *why* each gender values and prioritizes specific insights. The result is an unparalleled database of knowledge on gender, unequaled by any other entity today engaged in studying and reporting on gender issues.

Emerging from our data and shared in the first part of this book are eight gender blind spots—the leading false assumptions and mistaken opinions men and women have of each other and, in many ways, believe of themselves. In these chapters, we define each blind spot using our own research as well as the latest gender-based studies from research firms, consultancies, and leading universities. From our workshops and one-on-one executive coaching sessions, we share contemporary business stories of men and women caught in the blind spots, real-life accounts like Susan's and Bill's that bring the data to life in ways you can relate to.

Throughout our book, we engage head-on the huge debate over whether our gender differences are biological or social. Discoveries by neuroscientists, biologists, and psychologists have confirmed—without question—that many differences are hardwired into the brain structures of males and females and affect the way each gender processes information, rationalizes situations, communicates, makes decisions, deals with stress, and engages with the world.

In exploring the eight gender blind spots, you'll find the answers to the key questions we pose in our chapter titles, questions that expose both blind spots and their gender sources. Do men need to change, do men listen and appreciate women, and are they really insensitive? Are women being excluded, being too emotional, asking too many questions?

Women are not as content in today's workplace as men are. From the boardroom to the conference room to the call center, women feel valued differently than men. They feel dismissed for their ideas and excluded from events and opportunities for advancement. Men, on the other hand, are generally comfortable in today's corporate culture. His blind spot is in not being aware of how his behavior in this primarily male-designed environment affects women, while her blind spot is in assuming men's behaviors are intentional.

How we wish to be appreciated is often reflected in the way we express our appreciation, that is, we tend to give as we would hope to receive. For this reason, it's important to understand how men feel appreciated in order to understand why they don't often correctly express their appreciation to women. Men's blind spot is in assuming that women seek appreciation for the same reasons men do—an assumption that we'll show is misguided.

There are many "aha!" moments in our workshops, and what frequently tends to surprise many of the men are the challenges and barriers women face each day in the workplace—obstacles to their professional and personal success. Before long, the women begin listing their challenges, and we find the experience of being excluded most often surfaces near or at the top of their list. The men express apprehension and uncertainty, that they often feel they are walking on eggshells with women in the workplace. We list examples of situations in which men say they feel most uncomfortable and take extra care not to offend or provoke unwanted reactions.

We have, for so long, stereotyped women as "asking too many questions" to the point that today it seems men are more involved in curbing the inclination than in recognizing its incredible strength.

What never ceases to amaze us are the similarities in the challenges women face in working with men. Regardless of the country, women most often admit that their number-one issue is that men don't listen. Men are usually surprised when they hear this, and their standard response is, "Of course we listen!" Here you'll discover the differing modes of listening and how we can better communicate that others are indeed being heard.

And, yes, women are emotional, tending to express their joys, passions, and frustrations more often than men do. But does that mean they're *too* emotional? And on the question of insensitivity, we'll consider the differences in how men and women observe things, how they react to their environment, their concern for details, and whether the problem is forgetfulness or indifference.

In the second part of the book, Growing in Our Gender Intelligence, we share examples of how women and men are discovering ways to work together more effectively and, as a result, are finding personal satisfaction and a sense of fulfillment in their careers.

Throughout our book, men will discover ways of building trust with women, and women will discover ways of increasing credibility with men. Each gender will find ways to bridge their different values and complement each other's strengths while maintaining their personal authenticity. Women and men will discover how to gain greater work-life harmony and to reduce their stress both at work and at home.

This is not a paint-by-numbers book that will tell you what to do in every situation, giving you the illusion that you are fully gender intelligent. This journey is about increasing your understanding and personal awareness so the learning process will feel more authentic to you. This is about expanding your intelligence, making you more attentive, and deepening your understanding of how and why men and women think and act as they do.

Work with Me will enable you to peer inside the mind of the other gender and discover how to stop misunderstanding and being misunderstood. You'll learn how to put yourself in the shoes of the other gender, how to truly listen, and how to get your own message across more effectively.

Greater understanding can only lead to a greater appreciation for each other and the realization that our gender differences can be so amazingly complementary. Through the insights gained in this book, you will learn to stop the blame game, to see each other for the first time without blinders, to value each other, to want to work together, and to find greater success and satisfaction at work and in your personal lives.

Women and men in our workshops and seminars often ask how the gender blind spots that are so present in their work lives appear in their personal lives. Not only do they hope to learn how to be more gender intelligent at work, but they also want to understand how gender blind spots affect relationships outside of work. Throughout this book, we will offer brief glimpses into the *personal side* of life and explore how gender blind spots affect the lives of couples, parents and children, and dating relationships.

You'll also discover that once you are on this journey, you will want gender intelligence to be an ongoing pursuit. You will find yourself often asking the question, "Am I being gender intelligent?" You will forever seek opportunities to look deeper within yourself and discover ways to share your authentic self with the other gender.

Let's now begin this journey together.

ONE

ARE WE REALLY THE SAME?

LORENZO, AN INVESTMENT BANKER FOR OVER 20 YEARS, MANages a profitable branch office in Dallas, Texas. He has a great team of dedicated employees who enjoy working together. Judy, one of the two women on the team, has always felt a little uncomfortable with Lorenzo's occasional and slightly off-color jokes during team meetings as well as with his compliments on her attire, but she considers him a good boss to work for. She doesn't know how to give him feedback, though. She doesn't know exactly how to say it, nor can she predict how he'll react. "That could change the course of my career," she thinks.

Judy e-mails her human resources department in Houston, asking for guidance, and HR does its role by filing a report on Lorenzo and contacting the legal department. Legal along with HR meet with Judy, and in their effort to come to a by-the-book solution, relocate Judy to another branch—an outcome she didn't expect and Lorenzo certainly didn't want, as Judy was one of his top performers.

Judy's 15-minute drive to work is now a two-hour commute—plenty of daily drive time to reflect on what happened and why it all unraveled so quickly.

Needing to vent, she shares this story with her attorney friend. He suggests that she has a great case against Lorenzo and encourages Judy to sue the company. She takes his advice, wins the case, settles for an undisclosed amount of money, and retires.

Lorenzo is blind-sided by all of this. "I didn't know I was doing anything wrong. I didn't mean any harm." The company does the only thing it could do and fires Lorenzo. His chances for getting another job are impossible now with this sexual harassment charge on his record. His career is toast! He asks his personal lawyer if he has a case and ends up suing the company for not providing adequate training in sexual harassment. Lorenzo wins his suit and retires.

Lorenzo didn't know his words were having that kind of effect on Judy. It wasn't his intent to insult or "sexually objectify her," as was claimed in court. "I thought I was flattering her, making her feel good about herself!"

Judy knew Lorenzo never intended to harass her. She wanted to preserve the relationship and her job and not offend Lorenzo, but it just made her feel uncomfortable and she didn't know how to talk to him about it. Her request for support from HR set in motion a litigation machine that resulted in a costly settlement to the company, Lorenzo out of work, and Judy stuck in traffic.

WHY SHOULD WE CARE?

Considering the cost, many companies have every reason to fear a sexual harassment lawsuit. Complainants today receive, on average, $250,000 if she or he wins a trial. In addition, the defendant company has to pay all attorneys' fees. Settlements themselves can cost a company tens of thousands of dollars, but verdicts against a defending company can cost millions!

The U.S. Equal Employment Opportunity Commission has received an average of 12,000 sexual harassment complaints every year for the past ten years. Considering the pervasiveness of diversity training programs since the 1990s, you would think that number of complaints would decline. Each year, about half of the charges are dismissed with "no reasonable cause." The ones that do stick cost employers approximately $50 million annually.[1]

Then there are the personal costs. Companies adopt policies to prevent any chance of misconduct, such as prohibiting male supervisors from having closed-door meetings with women subordinates. Men are uncomfortable traveling or even having a business lunch with a woman colleague. They don't want *any* behavior on their part to be misconstrued. The sad irony is that the inability to meet privately or travel with the boss or other male colleagues can limit a woman's chances for developing her career.

WHY GENDER EQUALITY IS FAILING

The story of Lorenzo and Judy is real, although the names and locations have been altered to protect the truly innocent. But it pinpoints how truly blind men and women are to each other's intentions and expectations in today's workplace. There is no doubt that inappropriate behavior exists. Yet, so much of it is unintended—the result of misinterpretation and miscommunication between men and women, who have little idea why the other gender thinks and acts as it does.

In our gender intelligence workshops and through in-depth surveys of over 100,000 men and women on gender issues in the workplace for the past 25 years, we've learned it's not that men don't want to understand; they simply don't know *how* to read women's thoughts and actions. The same holds true for women. They tend to misread men's intentions and actions but believe they understand what causes men to think and act as they do.

In reality, men *and* women are often uncertain how to act with each other and how to react to each other. Many men admit they

GENDER FACTS[2]

- 9 percent of men say they "understand women."
- 68 percent of women say they "understand men."

don't understand women. Male behavior is more predictable, but not understanding or not trying to understand can lead to avoidance and not working well together. Both men and women are often hesitant to speak their minds or act in ways that feel authentic for themselves.

In our workshops, *women often say:*

- "Men tend to make quick decisions. I'd rather we discuss the issues more."
- "He can't look away from his computer when I'm talking with him."
- "I like to ask questions. It doesn't mean I'm uncertain or uncommitted."

Men often say:

- "I'm often at my best when I can think and work alone."
- "The women on our team ask a lot of questions that often slow down progress."
- "I tend to hold back on giving women critical feedback."

One major problem is that we're trying too hard to be "equal" to each other, which, over the years, has grown to mean "acting the same." Since the equality movement that began in the early 1970s, we have been conditioned to believe that men and women think and act alike—but after 40-plus years, it's clearly not working for us. We don't feel valued or appreciated for who and what we are. We have difficulty getting our point across. We may mean well, but we're often misunderstood.

We are suppressing our true natures and trying to act the same instead of acting as ourselves. We've been encouraged to compete with each other rather than to find ways that complement each other, and this is creating unnecessary stress and unhappiness in our work life and personal life.

The fact is men and women are different. We do almost everything differently. We communicate, solve problems, prioritize, make decisions, resolve conflicts, handle emotions, and deal with stress differently.

One of most insightful sessions in our workshops is when women and men break into separate groups and identify their top challenges in working with the other gender. There are seldom any challenges mentioned when they're together, but separate them and in short order the list begins. The interesting thing is, regardless of the country, the challenges that men and women have in working with each other are virtually the same. Men and women the world over share similar patterns of attitudes and behaviors, notwithstanding their upbringing, education, or culture.

This idea of gender equality is not working anywhere—not even in gender-progressive Scandinavia, home to some of the most advanced, gender equal countries in the world. Norway, for example, was an early adopter of legislation to force companies to recruit women for the boardroom. Since the 1980s, these countries have led the way in gaining more rights for women, including the option of the most flexible work schedules of all other developed nations. Yet, Nordic countries are today below the global average in percent of women in senior management.[3]

It's easy to proclaim that "we're all equal" and go about treating each other the same, but when the dust clears, men and women are still misunderstanding each other and being misunderstood. We're not valuing each other and we're even further away from finding the complement in each other.

WE ARE NOT THE SAME

Since the 1990s, researchers in neuroscience have made great strides in identifying gender differences in human brain anatomy, chemical processes, and functions. Brain studies of more than a million participants in over 30 countries have shown conclusively how physiological differences in the male and female brains influence language, memory, emotion, vision, hearing, and spatial orientation.

Although we are biologically different, this does not mean that one sex is superior or inferior to the other. Yet, even in the face of so much scientific evidence, there are many who firmly believe that, aside from physical appearance and reproductive capabilities, males and females are the same. They maintain that gender differences in attitudes and behaviors are purely the result of socialization in male-dominated societies, and that this oppressive domination over the generations has relegated women to specific caregiving roles. It's as if being biologically different than men can only mean being weaker or inferior. In their manner of thinking, science is being used to justify keeping women in lower-value, or "care-giving" roles.

We agree that there has been and still is oppression in the world—from the subtle to the brutal. Consider this: more girls have been killed in the last fifty years—particularly in China, India, and Pakistan—simply because they were girls than the number of men killed in all the wars of the twentieth century.[4] We believe that a great deal of the undervaluing of women in this world exists because of the lack of "gender intelligence."

Gender intelligence is an active consciousness that views gender differences as strengths, not weaknesses. It is an understanding that both nature and nurture play a significant role in a person's life. The extent to which our differences are informed by our biology or by family, education, and culture is not a question that can easily be answered, simply because there is no general formula that can be applied to everyone equally. The balance of biology and social influence is unique to every individual and situation.

By continuing to believe that gender differences are all or even predominantly due to social influence is to deny our nature. We've been conditioned to believe that men and women are the same. We often over-expect the opposite gender to think and act the same, and we often undervalue the differences when they show up.

WE OVER-EXPECT SIMILARITIES

Of the eight gender blind spots in this book, the belief of "sameness" is the greatest obstruction to our improved vision of each other. It's the foundational assumption underlying most of the false expectations men and women have of each other and the source of nearly all of our misunderstandings and miscommunications.

Despite the fact that today women make up half of middle management in pretty much every industry, the working world they've entered has been designed—for the most part—by men for men. Men are, by and large, very comfortable in this environment and generally don't see any need for change. It's often uncomfortable for women who have little choice but to adapt to the male style of work.

Men didn't intentionally plan this as a way of keeping women out. It's just that when the corporate structure was developed generations ago, the majority of the workforce was comprised of men. As a result, men have written the basic rules of engagement in business and made them more effective and efficient over the years—from leading teams, to conducting meetings, to prioritizing issues, to making decisions. Even how and where to socialize after work—from golf outings to gentlemen's clubs—is based on men's preferences.

During our workshops, men are often asked to reflect on and share their unspoken rules, the policies and procedures they would never think about if not asked. Here's a composite of what men tend to identify as codes for their behavior. Further, the rules of engagement at the workplace are virtually the same, whether the workshops are held in Denver, Denmark, or Dubai.

- "The effort of everyone working together is important, but it's the results that matter most."
- "To offer a man support is to suggest that he's incapable. To let him work it out by himself makes him stronger. If he needs help, he'll ask."
- "If a man is sitting quietly in meeting, don't put him on the spot by asking, 'What do you think?' If he has something to say, he'll say it on his own."
- "Don't show emotion. It means you're weak. Remain calm and confident."
- "Business is business. Don't make it personal or take it personally."

It's hard for men to want to improve on their rules. Why would they want to? They feel authentic and motivated in their environment, which reveals another big rule with men: "If it isn't broken, don't fix it."

Women, entering this workplace, struggle and find it hard to adjust. They would rather the workplace adjust to them so they can feel authentic and motivated:

- "The journey is as important as the destination. Improving performance achieves the goal."
- "To offer a woman support makes her feel included and allows her to give back."

- "Women want to be asked, 'What do you think?' It invites them to share their ideas."
- "A show of emotion is not a show of weakness. Emotion is a source of strength and often passion."
- "Women tend to take it personally and internalize the issue: 'What could I have done better?'"

Men know the rules, they live by them every day, and they generally expect women to play by the same rules. Men aren't being intentionally exclusive or indifferent, they just don't know what they don't know.

For far too long, the "we're all the same" solution to this has been that women adopt male behavior to fit in and advance in the male hierarchy. The majority of training programs, workshops, seminars, and books have been devoted to training women to think and act like men in order to succeed. Examples of these male-behavior training activities are shared in the chapters to follow. One describes a series of assertiveness training programs designed for women executives in Silicon Valley in California in early 2000, training that brought out their aggression instead of their assertiveness.

"I SEE ONLY ONE MODEL OF LEADERSHIP HERE!"

A woman CEO candidate for a Fortune 100 company attends a very expensive four-day leadership training course offered by a prestigious university in the northeastern United States. The course has been offered to executives in business and government for over 30 years and over the years has made slight updates to the materials with new case studies and leadership traits development.

The CEO candidate and instructor are talking before the first day of classes begins and the woman says, "I've noticed that the men and women on my staff practice their leadership differently. Will we be exploring gender differences in leadership over the next four days? Almost half the attendees are women. I see only one model of leadership here. And there are more individual than group assignments."

The instructor replies, "Our focus will be on the principles of sound leadership, such as having a vision, showing integrity, taking responsibility, building trust, and being goal driven. These principles are shared by men and women alike."

She thinks to herself: "I show my integrity and build trust in different ways. And being goal driven is not my only focus. I *share* my leadership. These four days are not designed for that."

And she's correct. McKinsey & Company's recent survey of 9,000 leaders from around the world, measuring the frequency of use of the Nine Leadership Behaviors That Improve Organizational Performance, revealed that women and men show different though complementary leadership strengths:[5]

TABLE 1.1

Gender Strength	The Nine Leadership Traits
Women apply more than men	• people development • expectations and rewards • role modeling
Women apply slightly more than men	• inspiration • participative decision making
Women and men apply equally	• intellectual stimulation • efficient communication
Men apply more than women	• individual decision making • control and corrective action

The five behaviors that women apply more or slightly more than men—people development, expectations and rewards, role modeling, inspiration, and participative decision making—have become increasingly critical in attracting and retaining talent and in creating an ensemble form of leadership to succeed in a global and diverse marketplace.

Seventy percent of the CEOs of the companies surveyed in the McKinsey study admitted that the senior executives in their firms lacked those five specific traits. This stands to reason seeing as only one in five of those executives were women.

WE UNDERVALUE THE DIFFERENCES

When we present brain science research in our workshops and give examples of how and why our brain biology plays a large part in informing our thoughts and actions, it comes as a huge relief to both men and women alike. Their sense of relief is in the realization that there is no *wrong* in their nature.

The "aha!" moments are amazing as both genders realize together—for the first time—that their differences are not weaknesses but strengths that are misunderstood, undervalued, and often criticized. A great deal of work-life stress and a sense of being unfulfilled comes from trying to tamp down our differences and act the same.

The majority of people today are unhappy at work, and an international study by Gallup offers a good illustration of how low worker morale really is. The study questioned 1.7 million workers in 101 companies in 63 different countries. Employees were asked whether they "felt they had the opportunity to do their best every day" at their job. Only 20 percent felt they had the opportunity to put their personal strengths and talents to work.[6]

"I SPENT 15 YEARS CLIMBING THIS LADDER."

Sophia, the new senior vice president of global diversity for one of the largest software companies in the world, and Prianka, her vice president, spent a month preparing for their presentation to the board on their gender diversity plans for the organization. They are proud of their human resource team's creative ideas and programs that could position their company as the diversity leader in the software industry for the next ten years. They're excited by the opportunity to discuss the details of their initiatives with the board.

They fly to Europe from the west coast of the United States to meet with Sophia's boss, William, for the first time, and present to the board. The morning of the meeting, Sophia's boss informs her that he is going to present their diversity plans instead. During his presentation, William fast-forwards through many of the nuances and important points that the women had painstakingly woven into the plan.

The two women, sitting in the second row of chairs by the wall and not at the table, listen as the all-male board tears apart their presentation, then skips ahead to the timing and the cost of the plan.

On their flight home, the two women share their experience and what they could have done differently to create a different outcome. Sophia realizes it all fell apart when William said he was presenting. "He didn't have faith in me. He didn't think I knew how to present to an all-male board."

Had Sophia understood how to frame her conversation with William and pushed back by saying, "We devoted a month putting together this presentation, including weekends, and if you let us present, we'll do a brilliant job!" she might have gotten a different response from William.

Generally, a man hears "no" as "not yet!" whereas a woman hears "no" as "that's final." William may have assumed that if the two women really believed in themselves, they would have insisted on presenting the program. This is a variation on one of the male rules mentioned earlier. By not objecting and asserting themselves, the two women may have given him the impression that they were not ready or not confident enough to present to the board.

Men don't know how their actions are going to be understood by women, and women don't know how their reactions are going to be interpreted by men. A man assumes that the effect he is having on a woman is the same effect he would be having on a man.

If the two women who put the report together were men instead, William most likely would not have insisted on presenting their information. But if he did for reasons of control, the two men, knowing that they could do a good job, would have insisted on presenting it themselves and would not have taken William's insistence personally but competitively.

William's blind spot had an impact on the two women. On their flight home, Sophie told Prianka she was resigning her new position and leaving the company. "I spent 15 years climbing this ladder and sacrificing my personal life. We spent a month working on that presentation and 15 hours in the air each way, and we weren't even invited to sit at the table. I don't feel valued or appreciated here."

Without gender intelligence, men and women will never truly understand and appreciate each other's authentic, complementary nature. As much as men need to understand how and why women think and act as they do, women need to understand the same about men. Only through deeper insight, with blind spots revealed and removed, will men and women confidently and collaboratively work and succeed together. The model of the past—gender equality through sameness in numbers and behaviors—has only taken us so far. Gender equality in opportunity and valuing our differences will make us truly equal.

BY THE NUMBERS

Since the 1960s, there's been an effort to encourage more young women to enter college and complete undergraduate and graduate degrees. Some people believed that if colleges admitted and graduated more women, then the society would become more equal. Women would graduate, postpone marriage, enter into many fields, and advance into leadership in balance with men.

So where are we today?

Since 1982 the majority of U.S. college graduates have been women, receiving the majority of undergraduate and graduate degrees. The year 2009 marked the first time that more women than men received doctoral degrees—building on decades of change since the 1960s in the status of women in U.S. higher education.[7] Throughout the Americas, Europe, and Asia, women complete more years of schooling than men do, and in many countries a higher percentage of women currently attend colleges and universities compared to men.

Since the 1980s, women have held more than half of all middle management positions in the Fortune 500 companies. Yet, over that same 30-year period, the percent of women advancing to senior management positions has remained low and has hardly changed.

"AT THIS RATE, I'LL BE NEAR RETIREMENT!"

Lois had been a product manager at her technology company for 15 years before being made director of software product development. She had recruited college men into her department and within three years watched them be promoted right past her to directorships and then to senior management.

She shares with her friend one evening after work, "I put in more hours and have more responsibilities than most everybody in my department. I put my personal life aside and carried the workload for my team. I'll be near retirement before I ever make vice president."

"Unfortunately, the only way to move up might be to move out," her friend suggests.

"I like working with our engineers. They trust me representing their solutions and asking for resources from management. They'd rather solve the issues than ask for budgets, and I can understand that. It would be unfortunate for them if I left."

Today in the United States, less than 20 percent of senior executives are women, not very different from 14 percent in 1996. Less than 3 percent of CEOs are women, with no change since 1996. Globally, only 20 percent of senior management positions are held by women.[8]

For over 30 years, we have played the numbers game, attempting to tackle the problem of gender imbalance by forcing affirmative action policies and numeric standards on organizations. But these efforts are rarely sustained. Quotas often create resentment on the part of men, who view the process as unmerited and unfair, and frustration on the part of women, who eventually leave or stay and disengage, feeling undervalued and unappreciated in male-dominated corporate environments.

Many women are not experiencing happiness and personal fulfillment in their working lives, and these feelings are spilling over into their personal lives as well as creating a time imbalance. Their stress levels are off the charts with thoughts of many things to do and too little time for any of them.

Although men suffer a scarcity of time as well, they can isolate competing thoughts more easily than women can and focus on one need at a time. The problem for men is that the pressure to perform has created for many a perpetual imbalance in their lives, an almost singular focus on work. The source of stress for men comes from having to sacrifice their personal life, work long hours, and deliver results.

"THE MOUSE IS MY CHAIN."

At a recent workshop, Kevin, a first-time father, begins describing the joy of fatherhood but ends up explaining how difficult it is to find time for his daughter—already!

"I can't help but bring my work home. I'm competing for my job every day and I need the extra couple of hours after dinner to complete unfinished work. My biggest worry is never being able to spend quality time with my daughter and my wife, but I have to put that worry out of my mind and stay focused on the goal.

"I don't get it. My dad used to leave work at the office every night, and come home and spend time with the family. He golfed every weekend. I don't have six hours I can set aside just *one* weekend. But then, he didn't have a smartphone and laptop with WiFi. My computer is my ball and the mouse is my chain. I have to perform and deliver for my family. I don't mind, though. That's what's expected of me."

In 1980 in North America, only 25 percent of households had dual-career partners. Today that number is beyond 80 percent, and it's approaching that ratio of eight out of ten all over the world. There are two dynamics driving this steady and irreversible increase in women entering the workforce: economic necessity and the ambition of women.[9]

A VISION OF POSSIBILITIES

Mandating change alone or devising recruitment plans that will "double the percent of women in senior management within five years" will not ensure better results without greater gender intelligence. Companies that lead with gender intelligence—by educating men to understand the unique value that women bring to the table and educating women as to the reasons why men think and behave as they do—are far more successful in advancing women and men in unison. They are better able to sustain gender balance at all levels of the organization.

Companies that don't get it are being left behind. Young women today refuse to accept the barriers of the past. They want to live life to their full potential, and they will pursue their interests regardless of the obstacles. They won't tolerate being excluded or ignored, and they will seek out organizations that respect, engage, challenge, and promote their intelligence, talents, and skills.

"I DIDN'T EVEN MAKE THE SHORT LIST."

Before Hannah even sat down to our one-on-one coaching session, she explained, "in no uncertain terms," how trying to get her not to quit was a complete waste of time. So this was destined to be a post-exit interview. Hannah had just resigned her position as vice president of information technology for one of the top ten software development companies in the world. With her seniority and accomplishments, it was assumed that Hannah would be the next chief information officer, with her boss retiring at the end of the year.

"I was valedictorian of my high school class and got a full ride to Cal Tech in computer science," she recalled. "There were only a handful of us women then in the late 1980s, surrounded by young, very focused and intensely detailed men from all over, particularly India and China. I felt comfortable in the language and nerdy culture. I found them real. I wasn't as interested though in the pure programming as much as I was in the design and purpose. I was into the weight of their efforts—the social value.

"At the university, there was so much more collaboration with the men in the class than there is in our development teams at work. We tapped everyone's ideas and efforts and came up with the most elegant solutions. I felt included. We had each other's backs.

"I feel guilty leaving, but I don't see a career for me here. I didn't even make the short list of candidates for the chief information officer slot. Men outnumber women here 10 to 1, so even if I was given the position, I would feel I had won it because of my gender and not my accomplishments. And I can guarantee you, a lot of the men in my division would be feeling the same way. Yeah, *that* would be a great atmosphere to work in!

"A group of my college friends contacted me recently. They're forming a small company and are in line to receive venture capital for a new application they're developing. They want me to be the president of the company. It's breakthrough technology that the top three software companies have already shown high interest in. It's far less income for me now, but significantly more when we win these contracts—and we will win!"

We see this growing impatience and intolerance on the part of women on every continent. Today young, highly educated, and intensely ambitious Indian women show little loyalty to the companies that get in the way of their career advancement. Indian companies are having a difficult time retaining their female talent. Young women jump from company to company, looking for organizations that value them, provide the highest salaries, and offer the best career and advancement opportunities.

A BETTER MEASURE OF GENDER EQUALITY

The unforeseen consequence of 40 years of imposed gender sameness has not necessarily paved the way for greater equality between men and women. Most women today in our workshops, toughing it out on the front lines of their careers, tend to define gender equality and gauge its presence quite differently.

Although equal opportunity and equal pay continue to be highly valued (and rightly so as they are not yet universally achieved), women express gender equality as the ability to bring their authentic selves to work and be equally valued for the difference in their ideas, decisions, and leadership, not the sameness.

Gender blindness has successfully created gender blind spots—hugely erroneous assumptions on the part of both women and men that persist in the absence of truth. These blind spots are precisely what is causing our miscommunication, misunderstanding, mistrust, frustration, and resentment.

The only solution to achieving a cultural shift in attitude and sustaining any semblance of gender balance and inclusiveness is by understanding what is actually going on in the minds of women and men at work. That inclusion mindset—the essence of "gender intelligence"—is the recognition that men and women are not the same and were never meant to be the same. Personal authenticity is what builds and sustains gender equality—not women acting as men do and men acting as women. Our greatest strength—our equality—resides in our differences, and the true path to happiness and personal fulfillment is in understanding, appreciating, valuing, and embracing those differences.

What is fascinating is the number of studies today on the success men and women are experiencing in gender-blended teams. Behavioral studies show that gender-blended groups, in which everyone feels comfortable and all opinions are heard, are more likely to challenge established norms and get the best ideas on the table.[10]

This is not because men and women are so basically different or that women are more clever, more empathetic, or better than men. It is because women and men bring different viewpoints and experiences to the table and therefore add a richer collection of perspectives and values to the decision-making process.

In the following chapters, we'll explore each of the gender blind spots that prevent men and women from working and succeeding together. We'll explore the brain-science research that reveals how and why men and women think and act as they do. And we'll share stories of men and women wanting to better understand their coworkers, friends, partners, and children. These stories will bring us together and help us realize that we are not alone but are quite normal in the ways we think, feel, and act, and how we choose to work and desire to live our lives.

THE EIGHT GENDER
BLIND SPOTS

TWO

DO WOMEN WANT MEN TO CHANGE?

Women say: "There's room for improvement."
Men say: "If it isn't broken, why fix it?"

WOMEN ARE NOT AS CONTENT IN TODAY'S WORKPLACE AS MEN are. From the boardroom to the conference room to the call center, women feel valued differently than men. They feel dismissed for their ideas and excluded from events and opportunities for advancement. Women often sense that they have to work harder than men do just to prove themselves, and they feel doubted for their competence and commitment.

Men, on the other hand, are generally comfortable with the rules of engagement in today's corporate culture. They're not aware of how their behavior affects women, nor do they feel that they're acting intentionally against women. They just assume that women are prepared to engage in work as men typically do—whether the work involves prioritizing issues, solving problems, participating on teams, leading others, or making decisions.

Deliberately or not, men's and women's misunderstanding and misinterpreting of each other's meaning, actions, and reactions impedes their ability to work together in an authentic and productive way. Much of the time women don't realize men's good intentions, while men are often unaware of the value of women's consequential thinking.

"OUR DEADLINE IS AUGUST!"

Benton starts the meeting with a stern reminder: "Our deadline is August. We have four months to get our act together and ensure our hardware and software launch in unison. Mike, what's the status of our hardware engineers? Are they on schedule for the beta test in July?"

Mike quickly responds, "We have a development status meeting twice a week now. It's driving the engineers crazy, but I want to ensure we make the beta test date."

"That's excellent," says Benton. "Elizabeth, where are the software developers on this?"

"The developers are working really hard to make the beta test date." Then Elizabeth adds, "I think we have to involve customer service at this point. They think there's going to be a lot of questions from user groups and if those issues can be addressed now, we can save a lot grief in the long run."

The urgency in Benton's voice grows, "I'm not stopping our momentum on software development to address issues that may never come up. We have to make the launch date or we won't have customers to worry about."

The meeting adjourns and Benton walks back to his office with Mike and says, "I don't think Elizabeth is going to work out. I don't think she gets it. We need to make the deadline or we're all dead. I want you to sit in on her software meetings."

We discovered in our workshop that Benton had every reason to push for the launch date in August given that the competition was about to launch a similar product at the end of the year. Elizabeth was also right about potential software issues flooding customer service. The software performed well enough in the beta test, but the number of customer complaints forced a redesign within three months of the launch.

We all want to bring the best of ourselves to work every day. Yet, our false assumptions and misinterpretations of each other's thoughts and actions prevent us from achieving any real breakthroughs in understanding. These incorrect assumptions are even reflected in our data. A significant gender gap exists between how men and women view women's satisfaction with their jobs and women's chances for advancement.

GENDER FACTS[1]

- 58 percent of men believe that women have as equal a chance of getting ahead as men do. Only 24 percent of women share that outlook.
- 83 percent of men believe both men and women are experiencing the same level of job satisfaction.
- 93 percent of women believe men have job satisfaction. Only 62 percent of women feel job satisfaction.

WHY WOMEN WANT MEN TO CHANGE

Consider the social trends of the past several decades and you'll begin to understand why women not only want men to change, but *need* men to change in order to create a less stressful, more complementary working environment.

Two generations ago, for a woman to pursue a career may have been a choice, but today it's an economic necessity. Yet, the work environment that women are entering does not welcome the way in which women communicate, collaborate, and generally engage in business. When women say they want men to change, they are really asking men to remove the obstacles to their success and to value their contributions. This is not happening anywhere near the extent that women would like to see it occur, and as a result women often feel left out and undervalued.

In our Gender Intelligence Workshops, the most cited reasons why women feel that men need to change are:

- Women's ideas are dismissed and their concerns are ignored.
- Women feel excluded—from advancement opportunities to informal social events.
- Women feel they have to work harder than men for the same level of recognition.

Let's explore these areas in more detail to understand why women feel this way and why men are unaware of women's general discontent.

WOMEN FEEL DISMISSED

Women often feel their ideas and approach to work somehow don't carry the same weight or hold the same value or importance as the ways a man engages in business. In our workshops, women tell us about their experiences in meetings when they would raise an important point, only to have it ignored or dismissed by the men in the room. Yet a man will bring up the same point minutes later and everyone will give him their undivided attention.

Women commonly ask more questions than men do, not just for the sake of clarity, but to create an atmosphere of sharing and consensus building. Men, on the other hand, tend to isolate and eliminate issues in order to arrive at quick decisions.

"WE HAVE ONE HOUR!"

The client meeting is running much longer than Peter had intended. For the last 30 minutes, all he could do was watch the clock and think,

"We can't miss our flight." It didn't seem to unsettle Mary, his associate, though. Peter thinks to himself, "Why is she still asking questions?" He cuts her off in midsentence on the next issue she raises, saying, "Mary, that's not something we have to worry about right now."

Embarrassed, but trying not to show it, she glances over at Peter who seems to have been somewhere else for the last 30 minutes. "What's he so worried about? Can't he see that the client is beginning to notice his indifference?"

Peter is now speeding to the airport, not hearing a word Mary is saying as he plays out the next hour in his mind—"25 minutes to the car rental lot, 10 minutes to take the bus, 20 minutes to go through security. We'll never make it!"

"I wish you wouldn't have cut off my last few questions to the client, Peter," Mary says. "We needed that information and I wanted to see their reaction face to face."

"I didn't cut you off," says Peter, as he weaves in and out of slower-moving traffic. "I thought the meeting went well. It just went too long."

Men don't believe they're being dismissive. They're just doing what feels right for them and not thinking about the effect their actions tend to have on women. When a man hears a woman say that she feels ignored or that her ideas are marginalized, his first reaction is to reflect back through his own experiences to recall a time when he may have treated a woman colleague in that manner. When he can't remember an occasion or can't see himself intentionally behaving that way, he feels that he's being unfairly blamed for what other men may do.

Men want to work well with women, just as women want to work well with men. They both want to bring their A-game to work every day. But men and women think and act differently and don't understand why the other gender can't behave just as they would in the same situation.

In the spirit of expanding our awareness and giving voice to some of the discontent expressed by women, here are examples of how men unknowingly dismiss women by pursuing a course of action that may be understandable to themselves and other men, but tends to prevent women from participating in ways that work for them:

What men say	*What women say*
"Those issues aren't directly related. We need to focus on what's critical and doable now."	"Those issues seem relevant and may impact our decision. All things should be considered."
"Only two people have lodged that complaint, so I don't think it's worth our attention."	"There may be 200 others with that complaint. It's worth looking into the problem and resolving it."
"Let's make a decision and move on, or we'll be here all day!"	"I'd like to go around the room and ask everyone their opinion one last time before we make a decision."
"There's risk involved, but beating competition to the marketplace is worth it."	"To minimize the risk, let's think through the options one more time. We may not be first to market, but we'll have a solid product."

We're at an impasse when women don't realize that men's actions are not intentionally dismissive. And men don't notice how their behaviors, so much a part of the male-dominated corporate culture, cause women to feel that their ideas are disregarded. Men simply don't understand and appreciate the unique value that women bring to the table, and women don't know how to frame the conversation in ways that men can relate to and act upon.

WOMEN FEEL EXCLUDED

When women say they feel excluded, they're commonly expressing their frustration for being passed over for advancement, shut out of men's conversations before and after meetings, or left out of after-work get-togethers—the famous meeting after the meeting—in which important decisions are sometimes finalized.

Men believe that they don't intentionally exclude women. When given examples of actions that tend to exclude, men seem surprised and unaware of their behavior. They'll even try to recall occasions when they made an effort to be inclusive, just to make their case. "I invited her once but she declined. I just assumed she wasn't interested in having drinks with the guys after work."

"WE'RE PART OF THIS TEAM TOO!"

Mary Lynne, a senior CPA at one of the big-four audit firms, doesn't believe she'll ever move up in the organization, regardless of her stellar track record. As one of two women on her ten-member audit team, she describes her frustration this way—

"Sure, office meetings are important, but the real decisions are made afterward over drinks and cigars. I'm seldom, if ever, invited to those informal meetings. When Christine and I *are* invited, the men will be in their circle having fun, teasing one another, taking jabs at each other, and carrying on with their male banter. I don't deny men their opportunity to bond, but we're part of this team too. We don't necessarily want to join in their locker-room talk, but we don't want to feel left out either."

Men assume that women will not want to work in a male-dominated industry or company, move long distances for a job opportunity, participate in golf or other outings with clients, talk about sports or engage in male humor before a meeting starts, or meet after work for drinks. Some men say that they don't understand why they should have to give up their social events with the guys. They reason that women are more comfortable bonding with other women, just as they are more comfortable bonding with other men.

Here are examples of how men unknowingly exclude women by either not thinking to act more inclusively or by assuming they know women's intentions:

What men say	*What women say*
"He got the job because they assumed she would not want to move to Germany."	"She would have liked to have had the opportunity to make that decision for herself."
"Our annual golf outing has always been the best way to build relationships with our top clients."	"Since many of our client executives are women, we should offer other options to golf. Let's take a poll of our clients!"
"We guys just decided to have a few drinks afterward. We didn't think you'd want to join us."	"Let's plan some business social events for the entire team and not just guys only. Women make up half of the team now!"
"We were just talking about guy stuff."	"It's uncomfortable when men in the room suddenly go quiet when I walk in."

Men may react by saying that they too sometimes feel left out of a job opportunity, business decision, or social event. What men don't understand is that women feel they're being excluded solely because they're *women*. Many women tend to feel that way all the time. Most men can't imagine what it would feel like if they faced some form of exclusion every day of their working lives—regardless of their capabilities or congeniality.

WOMEN FEEL THEY HAVE TO WORK HARDER

Many women commonly feel that their male supervisors and male colleagues are continuously testing them and may even doubt their capabilities. Women feel they have to work harder than their male peers just to prove that they're deserving of the same recognition.

Men are often judged on their potential, while women are often assessed by their achievements. A "young male Turk" may be considered a "diamond in the rough" who just needs the opportunity to show what he's capable of, while a woman is more likely to be viewed as a novice who has not yet met the requirements for the position.

"TWICE AS MUCH, BUT HALF AS GOOD."

During a breakout session in our workshops when men and women separate to discuss challenges in working with the other gender, one woman explained what she means by having to work harder than men: "Sometimes I feel I have to do twice as much work as the men in my division to be thought of as half as good. Every day, I'm first here and last to leave. My business unit generates more output with fewer quality-control errors than any of the other business units, and our profit margins are consistently higher. The real measure is in our low turnover. We're a very time-driven enterprise and all the male leaders in the other business units can think about is delivering results. They don't realize that they're burning out their employees. We haven't had a change in our staff for two years. That means no turnover cost and training cost and fewer errors in production. That's one of the reasons our margins are so much better. . . . I'll never be considered for general manager. That would mean that my policies will be replicated across the other business units and I don't think the men will stand for that."

In our one-on-one interviews, men will commonly admit that they find it easier to work with men than with women, especially when it's with a person they don't know. Many men say that they understand and relate better to men, and some will even admit that they are generally more confident in working with men than with women. Men's tendency to prefer working with other men is particularly evident in traditionally male-dominated fields where women don't have as much of a long-standing presence, such as in fields of science, technology, litigation, manufacturing, automobile sales, law enforcement, or the armed services.

When men's dismissive and exclusive behavior may be more a result of instinctive thoughts and actions, testing and doubting the ability of women may be more culturally motivated.

What men say	*What women say*
"I think he has great plans for the future. He's a visionary leader with great potential."	"We should promote individuals based on their accomplishments as well as their potential."
"This has been traditionally a man's field. I'm not sure you'll be happy in it in the long run."	"More women are entering this field than ever before. Difference thinking will bring new discoveries."
"Maybe he should give the presentation to the board? They may be more comfortable with him presenting."	"Whoever can best present the information and speak to the data should be the one to present."
"I sense we're all working hard here. I don't see where women are being tested more than anyone else on the team."	"At times I feel I have to work twice as hard as the men in my group just to get the same evaluation and recognition."

In our workshops, women will express how they often feel tested at work and share that they sometimes feel that they have to work harder, longer hours, or feel that they have to outperform their male colleagues just to be acknowledged. Men tend to read this behavior the wrong way and assume women are working harder and longer because they may lack confidence and try to do too much to make up for it. Women, some men observe, "don't know how to draw boundaries and just walk away at the end of the day."

Interestingly, diversity programs designed to hire and promote more women than men in certain fields often add to this problem, prompting the perception that quotas rather than qualifications are the determining factor for hiring a woman into what may typically be a male-dominated field. Some women will tend to internalize the situation and begin to believe they got the job to fill a quota and forget that they arrived at where they are because of their credentials and accomplishments.

WHY WE'RE NOT HEARING EACH OTHER

Many books written on the subject of gender equality and women's issues give examples of how women are misunderstood and undervalued in the world of business. These books state that men are unconcerned about the inequalities faced by women or are intentionally creating these disparities to undermine women's success. These books will seldom, if ever, present men's points of view, or the reasoning behind men's behavior—motives that, below the surface, are not as deliberate as they may appear at the surface. As much as men need to understand how women think and behave, women need to understand the same about men.

It's completely warranted for women to believe that if men change their behavior, it will improve the working environment for women. But the solution may not be that simple. In our research and practice, we find that there are two fundamental, though related, reasons for men's behavior at work, both of which make it difficult for men to view the workplace differently and realize that a change in their behavior is necessary:

- A male-designed model of work.
- The hardwiring that influenced that design.

The traditional business model we work in today is so common and universal that men and women seldom stop to realize that the workplace itself is based on a male model of work and male code of behavior. This model makes complete sense to men because when men designed the corporation generations ago, the overwhelming majority of the workforce was male.

The structure and functioning of the corporation was initially fashioned after the military model of command and control. The result is a highly competitive work environment that rewards speed in decision making, individual performance, and goal attainment. This work model is conducive to the way men naturally think and behave, making it difficult for men to see their workplace and their performance in it any differently.

One would expect men to be more comfortable with today's work environment than women are. Men are more at home with the rules, processes, and routines, and they are simply unaware that any change it necessary. Men tend to believe that "if it isn't broken, it doesn't need fixing."

Women, on the other hand, don't feel comfortable with this model of work. It doesn't conform to the way women naturally think and act. For women, this command-and-control model is something that they have to endure and adapt to each day just to get ahead. This is one of the primary reasons that more than half of the women we meet in our workshops and seminars are considering leaving their companies.

The cold, hard reality for women usually starts after university, the last time they and their male classmates worked in an atmosphere of genuine team spirit, collaboration, and sharing before venturing out into the real world. Once in the workplace, most men quickly and naturally adapt to the corporate world, while many women, wanting to feel just as validated and accepted as men, find themselves entering an unnatural world that they would have designed quite differently if given half the chance.

Two different models of teamwork reflect the diverse ways in which men and women engage the world of business. Here are some of the different approaches men and women are inclined to pursue at work and within teams.

What men say:

- "I'm more comfortable with prioritizing and focusing on one issue at a time, otherwise nothing gets done if everything is always 'under consideration.'"
- "I rather work by myself and attend fewer meetings. I feel frustrated and stressed out sitting there talking when I could be getting stuff done."
- "I can get more done when I know what's expected of me and I have the independence to do my own work at my own pace."

What women say:

- "It's important to think of more than one thing at a time. There are too many interconnected parts and something will be overlooked."
- "My best ideas come when I can ask questions of others and have them ask questions of me."
- "The effectiveness of the work undertaken to achieve a goal and the relations developed along the way are as important as attaining the goal itself."

Both teamwork approaches are effective models; both work well.

But the workplace and marketplace have undergone tremendous change in the past 30 years. Today, the labor market is comprised of as many women as there are men. And the marketplace is no longer domestic but rather global and increasingly diverse. The centralized planning and decision-making model that worked so well in the industrial era is no longer the most effective way of leading and succeeding in the complex world of business today. The business design that dominated and guided the world of work and commerce for generations is giving way to a more collaborative model, a model more beneficial in this global information era—a style of business that is actually more aligned with the way women think and act.

When you look a little deeper, you start to recognize that the male model of work is primarily a product of the physiology of the male brain. The way men process work through individual decision making, singular focus, and immediate action parallels the way men instinctively process their world around them. And it's hard to change what's hardwired.

Though the male-dominated corporate culture is adapting to a changing world of business, men's hardwiring will not change as easily. Nevertheless, by understanding each other's nature, men and women can discover ways of working together that complement instead of conflict with the other gender's natural instincts.

When women or men are not being respected, appreciated, or valued in their working lives, there's a tendency to blame their organization's leaders or fault their colleagues. Given that women are entering a male-designed and male-dominated work environment, they are the gender that tends to feel subordinate and directed by values not of their own choosing or design. They are the gender that most often feels dismissed, excluded, tested, and doubted. As a result, the blame tends to fall on men.

If the situation doesn't change, women begin to realize that they're giving more than they're receiving. They'll no longer focus on the aspects of their work that they enjoy most, and their thoughts will tend to become more consumed with the rules, routines, and behaviors that cause them to feel discontent.

Over time, the things they initially valued about their work or their company—what first brought them happiness and a sense of personal fulfillment—will fade into the background and become invisible. Often, women will come to find that they appreciate their jobs less and some will leave, while many more will stay and disengage.

THE SCIENCE SIDE

Women, compared to men, tend to have a larger, deeper limbic system—the center brain that includes the hypothalamus, hippocampus, and amygdala, and functions as the hub of emotion and motivation. The hippocampus is where long-term memory is stored, and although it's less active in men, it's larger and far more active in women.[2]

Women also commonly have more connections to the emotional side of their brains and are more effective at processing and coding emotional experiences into their long-term memory and recalling and linking past experiences. As a result, women tend to have richer, more intense memories of emotional events than men, and they are able to make instantaneous memory connections to events in the past, which to men may seem like broad, sweeping generalizations.

Women tend to internalize and personalize their feelings. When under stress, a woman's mind can become flooded with memories of disagreements and arguments from the past.[3] When a man behaves a certain way, a woman will tend to remember all of his and other men's similar behaviors and conclude that "all men behave that way."

In a man's brain, the amygdala is significantly larger than that of a woman's. The amygdala's direct neural connections to other response areas in the brain allow men to respond rapidly to sensory input, focus on external factors, and take immediate action.[4]

While women tend to internalize, men tend to externalize, not recall past events, and concentrate on the situation at hand. They respond to their environment more quickly than women do because men's thoughts are not as filled with as many emotional connections to past occurrences. As a result, men have greater difficulty recalling past events or drawing similarities and connections as compared to women. This is epitomized in the response, "Other men may behave that way, but I'm being blamed for things I don't remembering doing."

The differences in the limbic systems of women and men have enabled each gender to instinctively protect and defend themselves and others for thousands of years. Women protect through reflection, connection, and cultivation; men defend through quick decision, singular focus, and immediate action—unencumbered by extended thought or emotion.[5]

"TRY TO TALK HER OUT OF QUITTING!"

Two things struck me as I walked into Elita's London office: the frenetic pace of work outside her office door and the look of stress on the face of a woman executive behind the desk of one of the largest software companies in the world. Her company considered her a brilliant and irreplaceable IT technologist, which is why her boss, Antonio, the European vice president of technology, asked me to meet with Elita and talk her out of quitting.

To gain a broader understanding of the situation, first I interviewed Antonio and his executive staff of women and men to determine what was compelling Elita to quit—the workload or the working relationships. I found Antonio to be an intensely goal-driven, highly competitive senior executive. He considered himself "balanced" in his approach to both the men and women on his team. Several times he referred to himself as being "gender aware," yet every one of the women on his team thought otherwise; they each felt overworked and undervalued. Moreover, none of the women on his staff had ever been promoted above director level.

When I sat with Elita, she got right to the point: "It's too late. I'm so gone! I love this company and my team, and I can easily handle the workload, but I feel I'm being used, and I know now that I'll never be promoted past this level. . . . Last month was the last straw. I had to take a weekend off of work for my young son who needed to have his tonsils removed. Antonio knew this, yet he called me at home on the weekend of my son's surgery. He didn't even ask about Ian, who was still in a lot of pain. All he could talk about was his so-called urgent request, which turns out wasn't urgent at all! Antonio just wanted to be one up on the Asia v-p of technology because the Chief Information Officer position becomes vacant this year. He was desperate to get his presentation in one day sooner than his peer! If Antonio gets the promotion, I know now that I won't get his job, even though I have the most seniority and the best 360-degree evaluation of any director on his team."

When I shared Elita's comments with Antonio, he was both stunned and upset. He had no idea she felt the way she did and professed that he had completely forgotten about her son's situation. I could tell he was embarrassed and becoming increasingly defensive. He reflected back over his engagements with the women on his staff and was hard-pressed to recall the times he "acted in ways that would make them feel uncomfortable or undervalued." Before I left, he showed me the paperwork he submitted earlier that week to human resources, indicating that Elita was to be his successor if he moved up.

IT'S NOT BUSINESS AS USUAL ANYMORE

Gender roles have changed dramatically since the 1960s, adding more confusion to our expectations of each other with every succeeding decade. It actually hasn't been business as usual for 50 years. Yet, men and women haven't really learned anything about each other in all this time and are still confused about what makes the other gender tick.

What we have failed to see is that we are not the same and that we remain gender ignorant when we force sameness on each other and expect sameness in return. We have to stop fixing women to act like men, then blaming men for acting as themselves. When we understand our differences, our language begins to change and our expectations become grounded in reality instead of assumptions. We become more gender intelligent and, as a result, we make more of an effort to understand, accept, and value each other, and we purposefully fashion a working environment in which men and women can succeed together.

Each time we ask women their opinions of the behavior of men in the workplace, frustrations tend to rise to the surface for many. Though women have plenty of cause to feel the way they do and to be totally justified in their need to be appreciated and valued at work, their generalizations that "all men behave that way and need to change" only lands as blame for men. And, when women say they want men to change, men tend to hear the message that they are somehow flawed. A man tends to become defensive because a woman's inclination to want to improve him surfaces as criticism.

Whether justified or not, blaming men generally does one or both of two things: it tends to shut men down, or they get very self-protective and argumentative. As we've seen, men will commonly try to find proof for why women's generalizations are not true, which increases women's tendency to want to blame men even more.

There is a more gender-intelligent way for women to express their needs and for men to understand and act upon what women are requesting. Communication is the key:

- Gender-intelligent women know to frame their conversations in ways men can understand. They realize men's proclivity to prioritize and to sequence their work. They're aware that men are all about performance and focus on the results more than the effort. Gender-intelligent women are also aware that men are open to learning if they see more effective and efficient ways of achieving their objectives.

- Gender-intelligent men are more aware of how their actions are being interpreted by women. They realize that women are just as goal-driven as they are. A gender-intelligent man also realizes, though, that women place as much value on the journey toward achieving that goal as in attaining the goal itself. A woman's tendency is to collaborate; her best ideas emerge while asking questions and having questions asked of her.

The more men and women grow to understand the differences in how they think and act and what informs those differences, whether instinctual or cultural, the more insights they'll gain into the other gender's motives. Women will grow to realize that men are often not intentional, and men will grow to realize that women engage the world differently than men do.

The more we understand each other, the greater our appreciation for our differences. And with greater appreciation, the more often we look for ways to complement instead of compete with each other's style of work.

THE PERSONAL SIDE OF LIFE: THE UNSPOKEN REQUEST

Women tend to believe that when something is working, it can most likely work better. A woman's nature is to improve on her environment and the people in it who are close to her.

This doesn't always work for men. When a woman tries to change or improve a man, his interpretation of her efforts is that he is somehow defective. He tends to feel unloved and unappreciated. He becomes self-protective and will tend to resist being corrected or told what to do. To offer a man unsolicited advice is to presume that he's incapable of thinking through an issue and accomplishing a task on his own.

A woman may have the best of intentions in her attempt to improve the person and the situation, but a man on the receiving end will tend to feel that he's being controlled and not being accepted for who he is and what he's capable of doing.

Often, the way a woman tries to change a man's behavior is to point out what's wrong and to express dissatisfaction indirectly and in the form of a complaint:

- "When you park your car on the right side, I have a hard time getting out in the morning. The other day I was late for work."

- "Suzie needs to be taken to her recital on Tuesday after school. You're home before I am and if you can't drive her, I'll have to ask a neighbor to take her and pick her up."
- "The kids could use some help with their homework after dinner. I can't clean up after we eat and help them at the same time."

When a woman makes the man the problem, it limits his ability to externalize the issue. It interferes with his capacity to understand what her needs are and to find the most efficient path toward finding a solution. But when a woman presents the problem as something outside of the man, he can view the situation apart from himself and effectively focus on resolving the issue for both of them.

Behind every complaint is an unspoken request. If a man needs to understand why he should do something, simply make the request. Rather than discuss the problem, a woman needs to present the solution that works for her:

- "Would you park your car on the left side rather than on the right? If you do that, I can get out more easily in the morning."
- "Will you remember to take Suzie to her recital on Tuesday? That would be very helpful to me."
- "Would you help the kids with their homework after dinner? That way, you and I can spend more time together on weeknights."

The insight for women here is not attempting to change men but to change their own approach in communicating their needs. Men want to be supportive; they want to be of service. They want to feel needed and appreciated. Men want to offer the best of themselves to their partner—they want to be the solution and not the problem.

A woman has to discover how, through her own actions and reactions, to bring out the best in a man—from his own best side. She needs to communicate what it is that she wants in a manner that works for him and that works for her. This will empower him to do the things in the relationship that he's no longer doing and even encourage him to get better at doing things, because he's learning and acting on her needs instead of struggling against changing his behavior.

THREE

DO MEN APPRECIATE WOMEN?

Women say: "Not by a long shot!"
Men say: "Of course we do!"

IN THE LATE 1940S, COMPANIES BEGAN SURVEYING EMPLOYEES in earnest, attempting to understand what motivated them to perform at their best and what they desired most from their workplace. A pattern emerged, revealing a formula for motivational success that became the underlying principles found in every management-training book then and taught in almost all training programs today:

- Offer employees a challenging job that aligns with their skills and interests.
- Give them the time and resources needed to accomplish the task.
- Allow them the autonomy to get the job done.
- Recognize and reward them for their accomplishments.

Back then, and for decades to follow, men made up the vast majority of the workforce, and these management principles wholly supported how men thought and behaved, how they preferred to work, and how they wanted to be valued and appreciated for their results. The "performance appraisal and review" process that became the gauge of an employee's work product is today still considered the standard for measuring an employee's accomplishments. The concept of a 360-degree evaluation was added to broaden the assessment, to gain input from subordinates, peers, customers, as well as superiors, but the theme remained the same: recognize and reward results.

Fast forward to this era of gender sameness, and the standing belief is that women will seek appreciation for the same reasons men do. Our data suggest otherwise—recognition for results alone works great for men, but not for the other half of the workforce.

GENDER FACTS[1]

- 79 percent of men feel appreciated at work while only 48 percent of women feel the same.
- 82 percent of women want to be recognized for *their effort* in achieving the results.
- 89 percent of men want to be recognized for *their results.*

With women comprising approximately 50 percent of the global workforce, it should come as less of a surprise that in Towers Perrin's massive Global Workforce Study conducted in 2007–2008, before the global recession, 80 percent of employees felt disengaged while 60 percent said they were "undervalued and taken for granted."[2] Disengagement ultimately leads to separation. Feeling undervalued and unappreciated, women have been "opting out" of corporations at twice the rate of men, yet this gender blind spot continues to conceal the underlying reason for that trend, and it is not because of work-life issues.

We recently conducted in-depth interviews with 2,400 women who left their leadership positions in Fortune 500 companies in a variety of industries across the Americas, Europe, and Asia, and uncovered the top five reasons why women were quitting, the least of which was for personal reasons.[3]

TABLE 3.1

Why Do Women Really Leave?	
Not valued in the workplace	68%
Feeling excluded from teams or decisions	65%
Male-dominated environment	64%
Lack of opportunity for advancement	55%
Work vs. personal life issues	30%

Women leaving organizations will often cite their reasons as "personal" so as not to burn bridges. Men believe they are hearing the truth, which perpetuates the myth that women's personal issues will usually override their seriousness about business or their desire for career advancement.

Contrary to popular belief, when women leave corporations, they're not opting out of business careers altogether. They're migrating to companies with environments that value their talents and skills or starting their own businesses, and they are doing so in record numbers.[4]

Here are examples of what we discovered in our in-depth interviews—reasons why women executives are leaving positions of leadership.

"IT'S NOT THE MONEY OR THE POWER."

Nancy walked away from her brand director position with one of the largest beverage manufacturers in the world. Her male friends thought she was crazy. "What are you quitting for? You're making great money and traveling the world. All doors open for you because you work for *this* company. What more do you want?"

Though Nancy's brand was the first in the industry to be developed exclusively for the women's market, she had no say over her plans for the brand's promotion or the creative process to market it. The company's chief marketing officer and his two male vice presidents had complete control over her brand. The company didn't want to risk a product failure. What began as a great opportunity for Nancy to nurture the positioning and growth of her product became a frustrating daily grind. All of her attempts to influence the marketing effort were ignored.

"THEY REFER TO MY TEXTBOOK, BUT NOT TO ME!"

Madhu is considered a top pediatrician in India, working for one of the finest pediatric hospitals in that country. Out of a staff of 20 pediatric specialists, Madhu is one of only two women—not surprising considering the decades of restrictions on women entering the field of medicine in that country.

Although almost a third of medical students in India today are women, hospitals are still run by male doctors, many of whom hold firmly to the traditions of the past, which is why Madhu is resigning her position at the hospital and starting a private practice in the United Kingdom. "I'm at the top of my field," says Madhu. "I've even authored a best-selling book on children's medicine used in the majority of hospitals in India today, but the male staff here continues to isolate me. It doesn't make any sense. I can't speak my mind or influence the way pediatric medicine is practiced here. They refer to my textbook, but not to me!"

"WE NEED RESULTS, NOT VALUES."

Most everyone in the company assumed Shirley would be a succession candidate for chief executive officer. She not only had the seniority and credentials, but also she had the admiration of her staff and the respect of hundreds of employees who worked for her indirectly. Shirley even wrote the values that the company adopted three years ago—values that defined the vision of the organization; the consideration and appreciation company leaders would show their employees; the respect employees would show each other; and the care and concern the company would extend to its customers, suppliers, and vendors.

"Not being named a candidate for the CEO position hurts in a way, but I would still be willing to stay here," Shirley said in her post-exit interview. "What changed my mind is the statement the current CEO recently made during an executive team meeting. He said that 'given the state of the economy and declining sales, values mean nothing and that results and results alone will become the focus of the organization.' . . . If he were truly retiring, I would stay, but he intends to remain the board chair and I simply don't agree with his philosophy. Nor will the majority of women who work here who believe that valuing each other and working together is what will guarantee the results."

How we wish to be appreciated is often reflected in the way we express our appreciation; that is, we tend to give as we would hope to receive. For this reason, it's important to understand how men feel appreciated to understand why they don't effectively express their appreciation to women.

HOW MEN FEEL APPRECIATED

Men appreciate being acknowledged for their results. For men, it's not so much the journey or the efforts undertaken while achieving their objectives, but the successful completion of the task itself. For many men, a paycheck at the end of the month is all the appreciation they need! "Just let me do my job and I'll deliver all day long."

Men appreciate having the freedom to make their own decisions, not being micromanaged during the process of achieving their objectives, and having the latitude to make mistakes and learn from their errors.

What detracts from a man's sense of independence is offering him unsolicited help. It indicates to a man that he is not trusted or capable of accomplishing the job on his own. Because of this "I can do it by myself" attitude, men will leave other men alone. Also, because men tend to prefer to fix things or solve problems by themselves, they assume others—whether men or women—prefer to be left alone as well.

"I DON'T THINK SHE LIKES ME WORKING ALONE."

James is a creature of habit. He parks in the same space every morning well before 9 A.M., grabs a coffee from the cafeteria, and makes a bee-line to his cubicle where he prepares asset, liability, and capital account entries all day. All of the company's business-unit leaders consider James an accounting wiz, and his daily routine is often interrupted with phone calls from company leaders with budgeting or invoicing problems. He listens to their issues and recommends financial actions and accounting options.

Marjorie, a CPA recently hired by the company, is now James's boss. James enjoyed working for Steven, who was recently promoted to controller for the company. What James enjoyed most was that Steven hardly ever met with James, aside from conducting quarterly performance reviews, which were always stellar. "Steven trusted me to do my job. He never micromanaged me," James reflected.

"Things are different now. I don't think Marjorie wants me working alone. I have to meet with her each morning and she's talking about hiring an assistant to help me. I don't need help. She either doesn't trust me or doesn't think I'm following accounting principles. I don't know what it is. Maybe she's looking to replace me?"

Men genuinely believe they are showing appreciation, encouragement, and trust by letting others do their own work and in their own way—as long as they successfully complete the task. Male coworkers and bosses would never think of offering assistance to a peer or a direct report unless he or she specifically asked for help.

This goes to the heart of why men may, deep down inside, appreciate women but fail to show their appreciation and support in ways that women would expect and value. The kind of appreciation and support that women want and expect is simply not the kind of appreciation and support that many men would ever want to receive for themselves, so men simply don't think to offer it.

HOW WOMEN FEEL APPRECIATED

While men thrive on recognition for their results, women feel most appreciated and validated when they're acknowledged for the challenges they faced in attaining those results. We've said it before but it bears repeating: to most women, experiencing their journey is as valuable as arriving at their destination.

In addition, women tend to be relationship-oriented. They tend to be more personally interested in others and demonstrate their interest and caring by asking informed questions. Questioning and sharing are how women express appreciation for others and expect appreciation from others in return. Thus, women generally approach projects collaboratively and cooperatively, while men tend to engage in work independently and competitively.

This is such a stark difference! While men consider being questioned or offered unsolicited support to be signs of mistrust and lack of confidence in their abilities, women tend to feel the exact opposite. They consider questions, the unsolicited support of others, and the open sharing of ideas a sign of trust and an opportunity to establish a balanced relationship.

This is often very difficult for men to understand. Men tend to think that women should feel appreciated simply because they have responsibility, a good salary, opportunity to earn more, and the chance to move up in the company. Men don't realize that for many women, a collaborative work environment, peer and supervisory support, and building sharing and reciprocal relationships are as important as money, status, and power.

It's common for women to seek understanding before taking action. For this reason, communication to a woman is of primary importance. Making sure everyone on a team or in a meeting has an opportunity to share his or her ideas and to feel heard is important to finding the solution to a problem.

The clear differences in how men and women prefer to work and how they want to be acknowledged and appreciated for their efforts can be compared below.

How men feel appreciated	How women feel appreciated
Being singled out to accomplish a task	Being chosen as part of a team to accomplish a task
Being left alone as a sign of confidence and trust and an opportunity to show what he can do	Receiving unsolicited support as a sign of trust and establishing a sharing relationship with others
Not being asked questions during the process so he can concentrate on a solution	Being asked questions throughout the process to collaborate and discover solutions with others
Being allowed to compete during meetings to show personal ability and outdo rivals without acknowledging the contribution of others	Being allowed to participate during meetings through an open and balanced sharing of ideas while acknowledging everyone's contribution
Being acknowledged and rewarded for the results	Being recognized for the challenges and contributions along the way as well as rewarded for the results

There are many reasons why women seek appreciation differently than men, and although some of those differences result from upbringing or social conditioning, there are physiological differences in the brain structures and hormonal chemistry of men and women that influence each gender's need for and reaction to recognition. Acknowledging these hardwired differences helps us to understand how unrealistic our

THE SCIENCE SIDE

The inferior parietal lobule (IPL) is the part of the brain that receives signals representing the sensation of touch, self-perception, and vision, and it integrates these signals that enable an individual to determine identity, direction, and meaning.[5]

Research finds that men tend to use one side of their brain (particularly the left side for verbal reasoning) while women tend to use both cerebral areas for visual, verbal, and emotional responses. These differences in brain use underlie the difference in learning and behavior between men and women.[6]

The IPL is often larger on the left—or logical, analytical, and objective—side of the brain In men, prompting them to be action-oriented with high focus on task and achievement. Men are inclined to measure themselves by what they accomplish. They feel great comfort and stimulation when solving problems in isolation and in sequence, and respond well when acknowledged for their performance.

Men tend to focus on the most effective and efficient means of getting from point A to point B, what the outcome will be as a result of their efforts, and if that outcome is worth achieving. As an example, in business meetings, men will tend to stick to an agenda and move through all the listed items in order, checking each item off as completed as they systematically work through the schedule.

In women, the IPL is often larger on the right—or intuitive, thoughtful, and subjective—side of the brain. Women are inclined to measure themselves by their successes in relationship-building and knowledge-sharing. They commonly feel greater comfort and stimulation In engaging with others and respond better when acknowledged for their skill in collaborating and creating meaningful and productive alliances.

A woman's priority is not so much finding the most efficient path to accomplishing a task as it is building relationships that support collaboration and result in achieving an objective together as a team.

When men are in their natural flow of focused and sequential concentration, they commonly dislike the interruptions of open-ended questions and additional considerations, which women tend to offer in their effort to achieve greater understanding of a problem or opportunity. Women feel dismissed when men are absorbed in their pattern of thinking. They feel locked out and unable to contribute in ways that provide greater meaning and value and allow them to arrive at what they believe will result in a better conclusion.

These differences are not black and white, and there are exceptions to every rule. It is easy to find women who prefer to think and work in sequential focus and men who search for context and value collaboration. Without a doubt, social conditioning and natural temperament also play a part in defining who we are and how we think and behave as individuals. Nevertheless, biological gender differences have been shown to be true in scientific studies based on large, diverse populations of men and women.

---

expectations are that women and men should always think and act alike. Recognizing that many of our differences are biological releases us from believing that we need to think and act the same. It also frees us to find ways to respect and value our differences when they do appear.

HOW MEN FALL SHORT

Men tend to thrive on competition while women are often more acknowledging and appreciative of others, many times to the point of self-sacrifice. Consider the difference in this teamwork example:

The team leader walks into the conference room and asks, "Who completed the project?"

- Selma, the project coordinator says, "Carol did."
- Carol responds by saying, "Actually, Pritha got most of it done last night after work."
- Pritha quickly responds, "I couldn't have done it without your help, Carol!"

The women on the team will go back and forth acknowledging each other, almost to the point of competing to see who can acknowledge the other more! It may take a while for the team leader to discover who finished the project. None of the women will step up and take credit without giving credit first.

Now let's view this in a parallel universe:

The team leader walks into the conference room and asks, "Who completed the project?"

- Jim, the project coordinator says, "I finalized the project plan last night and we have a pilot now."
- Liam responds, "Yeah, I got engineering to complete the prototype on time."
- Gabriel adds, "I convinced our largest customer to run the pilot for six months."

Each of the men will take as much credit as they can and none of them will feel unappreciated by the other because, in a way, their nature is to appreciate themselves. It's part of the male ritual, and men tend to get along very well together in this practice. They enjoy working together and understand each other.

For many men, teamwork is similar to playing a competitive sport. They are continuously trying to take the ball from each other and score. It's perfectly fine because it's in the rules to take the ball and run with it and add to the total score—as long as the game is played fairly.

Bring men and women together into a team and we begin to see the clash of expectations in the absence of understanding. One of women's greatest complaints that emerge from our data is in not feeling appreciated when they bring up an idea during a meeting. The tendency is for a man to take the idea, make a few adjustments, and own it as his idea. The next man across the table will add to the "tossed up" idea and own it back, and this will go back and forth until they move on to the next item on the agenda.

To the woman who originated the idea, this all feels somewhat egotistical. She's waiting for someone to acknowledge her, but she could wait all day and that may not happen, leaving her feeling some-what marginalized and unvalued. Unlike men, women often are not in their comfort zone by acknowledging themselves. Their natural in-clination is to act inclusively, to take balanced turns in talking, and to acknowledge the ideas of others.

"HOW *I* SHOT THE BEAR."

In 1996, Xerox's company-wide sales goal was to beat Canon, their number-one competitor. The vice president of sales had camouflage T-shirts made up for the sales team, which was comprised of men and women, with BEAT CANON in big, bold letters emblazoned across the front. The stretch goal was to sell more photocopy machines than Canon in the first two quarters of that year.

Xerox was successful in outselling Canon in those first six months, and during the awards banquet when the sales team received their recognition and awards from the vice president of sales and other company officers, it wasn't difficult to notice the different reactions of the men and women on the team. The men were high-fiving each other with each taking credit for their part in the win through how-*I*-shot-the-bear success stories. The women on the sales team were more other-oriented in their show of appreciation, recalling the challenges and successes the team experienced as a whole, what *others* accom-plished along the way, and how they all "succeeded together!" They weren't as boisterous as the men or high-fiving each other as often as their male colleagues, although they were just as happy.

What was more telling and instructive of the difference between how men and women approach teamwork was that after a couple of days, the men simply moved on to the next challenge—the next hill to climb—leaving many of the women on the team expressing feelings of being left behind and forgotten. To many of the women on the team, something was lost in the exchange. Some described it as the loss of unity and ca-maraderie, a sense of being a team they had spent six months cultivating.

The men on the sales team couldn't understand why the women didn't show the same level of enthusiasm at the awards banquet and why they felt more regret than elation at the end of it all. The men saw the sales win as a tremendous accomplishment, and some could only attribute the women's dissatisfaction to "never being satisfied," which tended to build feelings of resentment on the part of some men.

When a woman shares with a man that she is not getting the appreciation she needs, a man will tend to tune out or roll his eyes, which makes her feel unappreciated even more. A man's personal thoughts or outward reaction might be:

- "She's not appreciating the opportunity that's been placed in front of her."
- "She seems ungrateful."
- "You got the bonus; what do you mean you're not appreciated?"

The blind spot for men is that they assume that women value the same things and in the same way they do. "The company gave you the freedom to do your work, the title, the office, the opportunity to make a name for yourself, all the things that I love and appreciate. I don't understand the problem?"

Certainly, those things are important to a woman, but what's missing is feeling heard, validated, and acknowledged for her actions. What men are not hearing is that what a woman *does* to achieve an objective needs to be acknowledged and valued as much as her achieving the objective itself.

"IT'S NOT THE MONEY."

Helen was an incredible assistant who ran the seminar company, handling all my clients, and paying all my bills. She was, without doubt, the dream employee. I didn't have to interact with her at all because she got things done. Her industriousness and competence freed me to focus on my work. I had confidence in her; I trusted that she was capable of handling anything that would come up while I was out conducting seminars around the world.

I appreciated her so much that I gave her a raise. A couple of weeks later, she came to me and said she was contemplating quitting. I was confused, "I don't understand. Why do you want to quit? I just gave you a big raise!"

"I know," Helen responded. "Thank you. You pay me very well, but I just don't feel appreciated."

I was really missing something here! I thought Helen was the best person who ever worked for me. That's precisely why I let her do her own thing—to show that I had faith in her. And I gave her more money to express my appreciation.

"How should I show my appreciation for you?" I asked. I had to know because I truly valued her work and honestly did not want to lose her.

Helen responded without hesitation, "You should know what I do in greater detail."

We both sat down and in ten minutes Helen was able to express her feelings, the nuances of her work, and the challenges she faced and overcame each day in dealing with our suppliers and partners and in managing my schedule.

I realized in those ten minutes that I truly didn't appreciate what Helen was doing for me because a lot of her work was invisible to me. I didn't know, but from then on I made it a point to know because one of the most valuable people in my life *wanted* me to know. Understanding what Helen was accomplishing on a daily basis and how hard she was working for me made me appreciate her even more, and it turned out to be a win-win for both of us. Helen felt appreciated for her work, and I grew to understand the support that was there. It opened up a deeper, more trusting, and more respectful working relationship between us.

The statistic cited at the beginning of this chapter is a reality for women—only 48 percent feel appreciated for their efforts at work. It's not intentional on the part of men not to hear or value women; it's simply a lack of awareness, which is why this blind spot exists. Men don't often recognize the problem. And if they don't see a problem, they can't express the proper level of caring or understanding.

FORGETTING HOW WE GOT HERE

The new CEO of a Fortune 100 company decided to make a surprise visit at the annual leadership summit to meet company leaders from around the world and encourage greater performance in the upcoming year. He took the stage and began by thanking everyone in attendance for their past year's accomplishments. "We all had great results in 2011 and I'm here today to ask you to dig down deep inside and aim even higher in 2012. We can do better! We can do so much better!"

The men roared and applauded spontaneously. They each felt appreciated for their individual contribution. The women clapped out of respect, but in looking around the room, it was easy to sense that most all of the women leaders in that ballroom didn't feel appreciated or motivated. They didn't seem as enthused as the men. From our vantage point, we caught many of the women glancing at each other with that polite, expressionless stare of disbelief. Two weeks later, we discovered why during one of our gender issues workshops.

A woman executive kicked off the session by reflecting on the CEO's speech that day. We knew she was speaking for each of the 25 women leaders attending our workshop because they each nodded knowingly as she spoke. "He didn't notice that the only people he motivated that day were the men in the room. Chanting 'we can do better, we can do better' is like pounding a nail into the brain of a woman. Women wake up in the morning *knowing* they can do better; we don't need to be reminded of it! It was as if the CEO was speaking only to the men in the room."

Another woman leader added, "We would have felt greater appreciation for what we accomplished in 2011 and more motivated to make the same effort in 2012 if the new CEO simply recognized all the hours of effort and personal sacrifice to generate those results!

"It was as if all that mattered was achieving the goal, then the next goal, regardless of what we all sacrificed to get there. That point was probably lost on many of the men that day, but I know it wasn't lost on all of them. Many women and increasingly more men are not feeling a part of the new, hard-driving culture of this company."

Not showing appreciation is one thing, but devaluing a woman by discounting her feelings or diminishing her worth are far worse behaviors that men tend to do without thinking. There are ways that men unknowingly send messages that tend to devalue women.

"I WASN'T COMPLAINING!"

Women will sometimes openly reveal their list of items that they hope to accomplish that day or week as their way of sharing, encouraging dialogue, and, in the process, relieving stress. More than likely, they're not looking for solutions or complaining about their workload. A man hearing this tends to misinterpret this rundown of tasks as a woman's sign of being overwhelmed or complaining, and he'll parachute in his solutions with statements such as, "Those things aren't important," or "Don't worry so much about it." He'll think he's helping to alleviate a woman's anxiety, but she hears something completely different. She will get the message that what she's doing is not important, and therefore she is not important.

She's trying to share the challenges she's facing—issues another women would understand and respond to accordingly and supportively. His statements, though perfectly understandable and acceptable to another man, tend to marginalize and devalue her thoughts and plans.

"OBJECTIFYING ME IS *NOT* APPRECIATING ME."

Men unknowingly objectify women by focusing and commenting on their appearance and behavior instead of on their substance and intelligence. Objectifying suggests that men are not valuing women for their talents and skills. It immediately depreciates women because it reduces them to an "object" or an "accessory."

Men, by and large, don't intend to offend. Many of the comments made toward women are almost reflexive and meant as praise. Much of this is learned behavior as boys, listening to their fathers compliment their mothers or the appearance of other women. Moreover, much of men's attitudes and behavior toward women is a reflection of how society has portrayed women in film, advertising, and magazines. The objectification of women is so deeply ingrained in our culture that it becomes difficult for many men to disengage from their learned behavior and equally value women in the workplace.

Many men do understand and are respectful of women, not just at work, but also in their personal lives. But even they will not break the male code by immediately calling out another man who is harmfully objectifying a woman. They may say something afterward, such as, "You shouldn't have said that about what she was wearing at the meeting yesterday," which doesn't break the male code because it is said privately afterward and isn't seen as a challenge.

Although many men have the integrity and intelligence never to objectify women, it takes a great deal of courage for a man to correct another man's behavior in public, especially in mixed company.

The new CEO of one of the largest management consulting companies in the world—a Harvard MBA graduate—attended the last few minutes of his company's strategic planning session one afternoon to review and approve the final plan.

To show appreciation for a job well done, he invited the team of four men and three women to dinner that evening. While at dinner, the small group began talking about the leadership styles and work ethics of the different managing partners around the world. The discussion eventually centered on the managing partner named Louis and his frequently off-color remarks. The CEO humorously recalled, "Yeah, I met Louis a couple of weeks ago. He doesn't understand that 'harass' is really one word!"

There was dead silence around the table. Stephen, the new CEO, this ivy-league graduate, had tossed a verbal grenade into the group of men and women, and Carlos, one of the male vice presidents, did an amazing thing and fell on it! He challenged the young CEO right on the spot:

"You know, Stephen, maybe 20 or 30 years ago, that may have been a funny joke, but today, it's not. I know I chuckled, mostly out of nervousness, but I'm uncomfortable with that kind of talk."

Carlos expected the worst now. Everyone could read it on his face. He had confronted and embarrassed the new CEO in front of the entire executive team of men and women, and was probably thinking about how much he could get for his home now that his career was over! The women looked at each other in total disbelief. The men stared at their plates and didn't move a muscle. The drama went up a notch as the red-faced CEO slowly rose from his chair, fixed his eyes on Carlos, walked over to the vice president, and in a voice everyone on that side of the restaurant could hear said, "Thank you, Carlos, I was wrong."

We so seldom see this level of courage in the breaking of the male code. A breakthrough occurred at that dinner meeting that evening, a breakthrough that dramatically changed the culture of a company.

Whether influenced by our different brain physiologies or by the social conditioning and learned behavior of our childhood and adolescent years, men and women are not the same in their expression of or expectation of appreciation. Women tend to express and feel appreciation differently than men, but through this false prism of gender sameness that permeates our society, many men are conditioned to overlook these differences and, as a result, often misinterpret the signals that women are sending out.

Our intent is to bring vision to gender blindness and shed light on the reasons for our differences so that men may open their minds and discover solutions on their own. We're also trying to help women correctly interpret the behavior of men so that they may recognize the support that's there and the well-intended but often misguided ways men are trying to offer it.

Without a positive understanding of how and why we are different, it's easy to misinterpret and incorrectly assess the other gender. We can easily slip into negative and judgmental thinking and project unsupportive behavior.

Only through expanding our gender intelligence can we begin to understand and respect our gender differences and learn to demonstrate and communicate appreciation in ways valued by the other gender and, in turn, acknowledge the ways appreciation is being offered.

THE PERSONAL SIDE OF LIFE: TUNING OUT OR TUNING IN?

After an emotionally complicated day at the office, where all of her new product-design ideas were completely co-opted by the two men on her team, Ruva looked forward to coming home, getting into some comfortable clothes, and eventually sharing her day with her husband. Vinay looked forward to coming home as well, lowering the garage door on the outside world, and finding a quiet space and time to regroup and recharge before dinner.

"Look, Ruva, there's nothing you can do about it," her husband said. "Those men were just building on your ideas. It's what guys do. You have to learn to roll with it and not worry so much. Besides, you're making damn good money. I *wish* I had your problems!"

Men are naturally motivated to communicate in ways that tend to reduce their stress, and Vinay would be in full problem-solving mode for at least another hour. Ruva, on the other hand, simply wanted to be listened to for just a little while longer. She wasn't exactly looking for solutions. All Ruva was looking for was caring, understanding, and reassurance. She wanted Vinay to respect and validate her feelings, and listen without judgment. Yet what she heard immediately transported her back to that conference room and devalued her even more.

This blind spot similarly surfaces when fathers and daughters communicate. The most common mistake a father can make is to offer his daughter solutions instead of listening when she's upset and shares something from her inner world. Dads assume their job is to fix things, when much of the time a daughter will just want to talk through her problems and be heard.

Many fathers are so singularly focused on providing for the family, they tend to be less involved in the day-to-day raising of their children. Often, this gives young girls the message that their fathers just don't care about them or appreciate them, when dads, deep down inside, really do care! When a dad does not show interest in the details of his daughter's life—her progress report, her friends, her winning her tennis match, or even her fashion sense—a young daughter gets the message that he doesn't care about *her*. Yet, fathers have a difficult time connecting because they express caring through action and not communication. To bond with his daughter, a father needs to put in the time by showing interest, by asking questions, and to practice listening without offering advice.

FOUR

ARE WOMEN BEING EXCLUDED?

Women say: "Let me count the ways."
Men say: "I don't know what you mean."

THE MEN AND WOMEN WHO ATTEND OUR WORKSHOPS AND seminars today are highly focused on achieving workplace harmony and building gender-intelligent partnerships. Our workshops are conducted in a variety of industries including financial services, high tech, consumer goods, industrial goods, health care, and utilities. Our attendees come from all levels of organizations including board members, C-level executives, managers, and individual contributors.

They often express frustration and confusion when working with the other gender, though they're resolved to find solutions. They attend our gender awareness sessions to gain a better understanding of why men and women think and act as they do and to discover better ways of working together. They are also hoping to understand how to channel new insights into their personal lives to build stronger, more enduring relationships.

There are many "aha!" moments in our workshops, and what frequently tends to surprise many of the men are the challenges and barriers women face each day in the workplace—obstacles to their professional and personal success. It doesn't take long before the women attendees begin their process of listing those challenges, and we often learn that the sense of being excluded is one that most often surfaces near or at the top of the list.

Men are often surprised when they hear what women say about feeling excluded, and the gender gap between men and women in response to this issue in our surveys proves this.

GENDER FACTS[1]

- 82 percent of women say they feel some form of exclusion—whether in business social events and casual meetings, in conversations, or in receiving direct feedback.
- 92 percent of men don't believe they're excluding women.

This gap in men's and women's understanding of the thought processes and behaviors of the other gender suggests that our conditioning over the years to ignore our gender differences and believe we're all the same has left us in the dark and continues to fail us. Men and women are not actively aware of each other's needs and expectations. Nor are we recognizing each other's unique contributions in the workplace.

Women want to be better understood and valued by their male colleagues, while men often find themselves confused as to the ground rules when working with women. Men engage in work in ways that feel natural to them and to other men, but their actions and male-oriented rules and procedures often run counter to the ways women think and engage with others.

A RECURRING PATTERN OF BEHAVIOR

A woman's feelings of exclusion don't stem from isolated instances or specific incidents, but rather from a recurring pattern of male behavior at work that tends to dismiss a woman's ideas and questions during meetings, prevents her from participating in informal networks, and impedes her chances of benefiting from valuable mentoring opportunities.

In our workshops, women often state that their voices are not heard in meetings and that their ideas or questions are overlooked or disregarded, unless restated by a male colleague. They recall some of the quick responses that men make during meetings that dismiss a woman's comments, abrupt statements that tend to discourage women from wanting to engage in further conversation:

- "That's a ridiculous idea."
- "What were you thinking?"
- "That's the last thing I would do."
- "No one is going to buy into that."
- "I think you're wrong."

Men tend to use these kinds of short quips with other men, who commonly don't think anything of it. It's an impulsive act on the part of men—their way challenging and competing with other men during meetings, often in a lighthearted way. Men tend to assume that women will receive these comments the same way men do, that is, by not thinking anything of it and simply continuing to toss ideas back and forth.

One of the major obstacles impeding women's visibility and therefore their chances for advancement is their omission from informal networks of communication—those casual situations and social settings in which team bonding takes place, introductions are made, one-on-one relationships are established, information is shared, and deals are often arranged. These informal networks and settings can include anything from client lunches to drinks and cigars after a meeting, to shooting pool, to golf outings. It can even include the occasional taking of clients to gentlemen's clubs.

Many of these networks and events are typically exclusive to men, primarily because they've been traditionally designed around men's interests. Women don't necessarily want to prevent men from engaging in male-related activities, but they do want to feel a part of the team and benefit, as men do, from the personal growth opportunities that tend to surface during these informal events.

TRADITIONS THAT EXCLUDE

Since the founding of the company in the late 1970s, all the men on the executive team of a Norwegian manufacturing firm rent a large cabin every winter on one of the many arctic fjords in Norway to go ice fishing for an entire week. This event is considered the company's most anticipated and valued business social event of the year.

For a month prior to the outing, the men will talk about their fishing trip before and after each staff meeting. They'll have lunches together and occasionally go out for after-work drinks to compare notes and take stock of the equipment they'll bring. Then, for a month or longer following the event, the men will continue to come together in meetings and lunches to relive how they "caught the big one" and make plans for the following year.

Women have represented 40 percent of the company's executive team for the past five years, but none have ever been invited to go ice fishing—though they would most likely decline the invitation. The problem, according to a number of women executives, is that women generally feel left out of meetings, lunches, and social events over many weeks. And when there are opportunities for advancement, the men will tend to support each other more than they will their women colleagues, primarily because the men have created a male-only alliance that grows even tighter and more exclusive after a week of fishing and bonding.

The men don't believe they're intentionally excluding the women. It's just that this ice fishing event dates back many years prior to when there were women on the executive team. In fact, the men will point to the five women on the executive team to prove that the company is inclusive of women. Nevertheless, this male-only activity has created an unintentional bias against their female colleagues by reducing their chances for advancing any further within the organization. Given that key clients are now invited to attend the fishing event, the women see this activity as even more isolating.

There's nothing wrong with men bonding with men. But apparently it has never occurred to company leaders to create a business social event that could involve every member of the executive team and not just men themselves.

MENTORING OPPORTUNITIES

Having a mentor is a crucial key to success. Personal mentoring has always occurred between men in corporations and organizations. A senior man takes a younger man under his wing, shows him the ropes, introduces him to important people, and eventually recommends him for high-visibility assignments. There simply aren't as many senior women in positions of power to guide the number of younger women coming up in organizations, and men tend to feel uncomfortable mentoring women one-on-one, for a number of reasons. One is that people tend to mentor those whom they feel comfortable around, those who remind them of themselves. Men more easily identify with other men, especially with younger men who are coming up the way they did. "He reminds me of the way I acted when I was in my 30s," is their often-heard comment.

Another reason men are uncomfortable mentoring women is the fear of sexual harassment, the fear of sexual impropriety, or the fear of what others might misconstrue. There's enough in this one reason alone to cause many men to avoid mentoring women. As a result, this type of executive-level support doesn't occur as naturally or as frequently for women looking to advance in their careers. As a result, women are often left to navigate the political waters of the organization on their own.

It doesn't mean that attitudes aren't changing though. There are many men with high integrity who are comfortable enough in their own skin to step up as cross-gender mentors, especially in companies and industries that are predominantly male. One insightful male said of his mentee, "Her courage reminds me of my own courage when I was in my 30s!"

"THERE WEREN'T ANY SENIOR WOMEN!"

Molly embarked on her professional career as soon as she graduated from college. Her first job was with an electrical engineering consultancy, an entirely male-dominated firm of consultants in a predominantly male-dominated industry.

"There weren't any senior women at the firm," Molly recalled, "so I did what I had done in college where there were only male professors in the engineering department: I enlisted the men at the office as my mentors. Looking back, my greatest mentors were the men I worked for," she said. "They didn't see me as a woman trying to prove something to men, but a person trying to make something of herself, someone who loved the profession, someone who was willing to work hard and excel at it."

GREATER SUCCESS IN PRIVATE PRACTICE

The flood of women into education in the 1970s saturated virtually every field of study, including law. The number of women receiving graduate law degrees quadrupled in the 1980s compared to decades prior. Considering the fact that women have received nearly half of the law degrees conferred in the United States for the past 30 years, there

	TABLE 4.1		
Year	Percent of Law Degrees Conferred on Women	Percent of Practicing Lawyers Who Are Women	Percent of Partners in Law Firms Who Are Women
2010	47%	31%	19%
2000	49%	27%	16%
1990	43%	20%	12%
1980	33%	14%	NA

has been very little cumulative growth in the percentage of women in law firms—at either the associate or the partner level.

Upon receiving their degrees, many women lawyers are not practicing law or staying in the profession very long, although that percentage has improved over the decades. If they do join a law firm, they're leaving after one or two years to start their own practices. In a broad study following the careers of men and women law graduates of Columbia, Harvard, Berkeley, Michigan, and Yale, the women believed—even more than the men who were surveyed—that women lawyers experienced significant barriers to their careers because of a lack of mentoring and exclusion from informal networks within their law firms.[2]

- 53 percent of women attorneys cited a lack of mentoring opportunities for women while only 21 percent of men believed that to be the case.
- 52 percent of women attorneys felt excluded from informal networks while only 23 percent of men recognized any omission of women.

Exclusionary practices on the part of men continue to hinder women's chances for advancement in law firms, but so do men's preconceptions that female lawyers are not assertive enough in securing and sustaining clients, aggressive enough in the courtroom, or committed enough to their careers.

Interestingly, client surveys measuring the depth and quality of client-attorney relationships, and juror surveys comparing the competence and credibility of male and female lawyers, tend to prove otherwise.

- The natural tendency that women attorneys have for listening to their clients is consistent with their *clients'* perception that women lawyers pay greater attention to clients and extract more relevant information about the cases than male litigators do.[3]
- Women attorneys engender greater trust by helping clients with emotional support and showing broader concern for their clients' needs, rather than by narrowly focusing on the legal case itself as male litigators tend to do. As a result, women attorneys, on average, retain more clients and generate more repeat-client business than their male colleagues.[4]
- Although studies show that jurors typically associate attorney aggressiveness with competence and view male attorneys as more aggressive than female litigators, a woman attorney who demonstrates her competence by having a command of the facts, law, and, when appropriate, technology, is more likely to gain for herself and her client greater credibility in the eyes of jurors than an equally competent male attorney.[5]

Being omitted from informal networks and mentoring opportunities over the years has noticeably diminished women's chances for advancement in law firms and as corporate attorneys, but it hasn't prevented them from finding success in private practice. Today women represent one-third of all attorneys in the United States, and the percentage of women in private, independent practice is growing faster than that of men. Women are not dropping out but finding greater success as independent attorneys and partners in smaller practices than they are in larger law firms or as general counsels for the Fortune 500.

"IT WAS NEVER MY INTENTION TO EXCLUDE YOU."

Women will commonly point to "men's club" behavior in meetings and at business socials and maintain that it's men's *intention* to exclude. A man, confronted with those comments, will recall all the times he was inclusive and respond with, "No, that's not true. I really did want to include you." He'll discount the claim because, in his mind, his intent was never to exclude.

Men, in general, want to find ways to work with women. In our workshops, men are often adamant that any omissions are not personal. Men behave in ways that are natural for themselves and understandable to other men, and they assume women want to be treated the same way.

Here are a few examples of men's often-unconscious actions, behaviors that seems perfectly acceptable to them and other men but that tend to invalidate women.

"He'll talk when he's got something to say."
When men are in a meeting and one man is not talking, the other men will respectfully ignore him. They'll assume the man quietly sitting there may not have anything of value to offer, at least at the moment. They assume that when he does want to contribute, he'll speak up on his own. It's a man's way of not putting another man on the spot.

Women tend to view team participation quite differently. They'll encourage everyone in the meeting to contribute, whether the other team members speak up or not. Women believe that it's proper and fair to include everyone, just as *they* would want to be included. A woman will therefore expect that a man will show the same respect for others as she does, and if he doesn't make an effort to include her in the conversation, she'll tend to feel neglected.

"We're just building on each other's ideas."
It's common practice for men during meetings to interrupt each other and compete to get their ideas across as quickly as possible. Men collaborate to compete and tend to approach teamwork as a team sport. One man will take another man's idea, make it his own by building on it in some way, and not feel the need to give credit during the exchange. In their free-for-all, men will continue to attempt to best each other as they "move the ball down field," then congratulate each other for a "job well done" at the end of the session.

Women typically collaborate to share and tend not to approach teamwork so competitively. A woman will typically give credit for another team member's contribution during the ideation process. When she's not recognized for her idea or her idea is taken by another man who then reframes it and makes it his own, she'll feel ignored and unappreciated.

"I was just kidding."
Joking is a way men test friendships with other men, allowing men to be critical in a light-hearted way. Once a man decides someone is his friend, no matter what that friend says or does—within reason—he'll still remain a friend. But there's more in this breezy kind of behavior than meets the eye:

- Joking is one way a man will react to making a mistake. He'll often externalize and deflect the error away from himself by saying something like, "It wasn't my fault!" Women, on the other hand, will tend to internalize the mistake with a personalizing comment such as, "I don't know what I was thinking."

- Men will often joke with other men as a way of bonding with statements such as, "That was a dumb thing to do!" Women, on the other hand, will tend to put themselves down to release tension from the moment in order to bond with another. "Oh, I'm always so late."
- Men also make jokes about other men as a nonthreatening way to offer critical feedback and test someone's friendship. If the recipient is offended by the joke, then he's probably not that close a friend or confidant. A man will then attempt to cancel out or neutralize the joke with the often-used phrase, "Just kidding."

Men, in an attempt to engage with women, will commonly tease and joke with their female colleagues the way they banter with other men. But that sort of humor tends not to land well with women and can actually have the opposite effect. A woman may interpret men's joking as an attempt to disparage or insult her. Men either don't understand this or forget themselves at times, and what may be a perfectly sincere attempt to bond and include is often misinterpreted as rude and discouraging.

MEN DON'T NOTICE THEIR BEHAVIOR

A man will sit at his computer, thinking that he can hear what the woman who has entered his office is saying, but he really cannot. He'll find it increasingly difficult to separate himself from the information on his screen. Even if a man is listening, he's only doing so with a fraction of his attention while he determines if what she's bringing up is more important than what he's working on.

Change the situation, and the effects will be quite different. A man who has entered another man's office will likely expect that the man at the computer is evaluating what's more important, and he'll tend not

THE SCIENCE SIDE

While men and women can reach similar conclusions and make similar decisions, the process they use for solving problems can be quite different and in some cases can lead to entirely different outcomes. Men and women generally evaluate and process information quite differently.

Men tend to focus on one problem at a time or on a limited number of problems at a time as they perform tasks primarily with the left or logical/rational side of the brain. They approach work-related issues with an understanding of the task and an ability to focus, uninterrupted, on what needs to be done. As long as a man doesn't feel powerless to complete a task, he'll engage in problem-solving, find a solution, and, as a result, lower his level of stress.

If he is unable to solve the problem, he'll typically shift his focus to the right side of his brain, causing the left side to receive less blood flow, thereby temporarily forgetting the problem that's troubling him.

This generally outlines a man's stress-response arsenal as one of fight or flight: he'll solve problems (fight) to lower stress levels or forget problems (flight) if he's powerless to find resolutions, which also tends to lower his stress levels.[6]

This is where exclusion enters the picture. Whether in focusing on and solving a problem or disengaging from a problem, men don't often notice that they're excluding others around them. They instinctively become distracted and self-oriented, set aside their feelings, and do not attend well to relationships while either solving or disengaging from their problems.[7]

Where men tend to use both hemispheres of their brain sequentially, women tend to engage in right-brain and left-brain activities simultaneously. The corpus callosum, a bundle of nerves connecting the right and left hemispheres of the brain, is larger in women's brains than that of men's and contains more white matter—nerve fibers that enable women to transfer data between the right and left hemisphere more efficiently than men. As a result, women tend to take in a broader, more inclusive perspective of a situation; they view the elements of a problem or task as interconnected and interdependent.

Women are usually more concerned with how problems are solved than with merely solving the problem itself. For most women, sharing and discussing a problem presents an opportunity to strengthen relationships, thereby relieving stress. Solving a problem can profoundly affect whether a woman feels closer and less alone, or whether she feels distant and less connected.

Where men's stress response is commonly to fight or take flight, women's stress response is to tend and befriend—to rely more heavily upon their support networks during times of stress, to tend to the problem at hand and befriend through communication and sharing. Talking through issues enables women to release the brain chemical serotonin, which helps them reduce their stress levels. Conversely, being excluded from dialogue tends to increase a woman's stress levels.[8]

Men's and women's biological models of behavior are not inherently constraining and are not necessarily absolute. They are directional in nature and generally describe how each gender typically responds to the world around him or her. Understanding each other's innate tendencies can help men and women recognize, appreciate, and respond appropriately to each other—at both the workplace and in their personal lives.

to take it personally. On the other hand, if the man at the desk is trying to determine if what he's doing is more important than what she's talking about, a woman will most likely take it personally. She'll start to believe that she's not important to this person who is so rude that he can't look up from his screen long enough to acknowledge her.

These small pattern like behaviors on the part of men are the kinds of things that tend to chip away at a woman's confidence and feeling of acceptance, yet they commonly go unnoticed by men.

DIFFERENT APPROACHES TO TEAMWORK

Men and women commonly define and approach teamwork differently. Women generally have a much greater need to be part of the team and regard teamwork as an opportunity to collaborate and communicate with others, a chance to build new relationships or reinforce existing ones.

Women derive personal gratification and support by questioning issues and being questioned and by sharing their discoveries and decisions with others. As a result, women derive feelings of acceptance and involvement that are typically not as important to men.

Men's tendency is to work independently until a task or issue is resolved. They generally view teamwork as a quick, agenda-driven exercise to confirm or calibrate a course of action, then to disband and go back to independent problem solving and individual decision making.

Inclusion is generally not a top-of-mind issue for men. As a result, a woman may misread a man's behavior in team meetings as being aloof and indifferent, which tends to amplify a woman's feelings of exclusion. Alternately, a man may misread a woman's need to collaborate, share, and question as a sign of indecisiveness and insecurity. He may even misinterpret a woman's questions as a show of suspicion or mistrust of his intentions.

During our workshops, we ask women and men what teamwork means to them and find two very divergent notions on the purpose of a team:

What teamwork means to women:

- "Share ideas with others and build on each other's ideas."
- "Build and maintain strong work relations."
- "Give everyone a chance to speak their mind."
- "Arrive at better decisions."

What teamwork means to men:

- "Assign and prioritize work."
- "Make sure there's no duplication of effort."
- "Ensure everyone is working as effectively and efficiently as possible."

- "Calibrate my work effort and allow me to get back to work."

During team meetings, men's general nature is to respond quickly to issues and form immediate opinions. They want to meet and disband so they can get back to work. Women, on the other hand, consider team meetings an integral part of work. They tend to take more time and consider all possible outcomes before forming an opinion and speaking their mind. Because of the time and consideration given, once a woman forms an opinion, it will be more rigid in her mind as being correct and immutable.

This is why women tend to assume that a man's quick statements are fixed and unchanging. Given that men's opinions are formed quickly and with very little input, women interpret this behavior as dismissive and exclusionary. She'll tend to assume that he doesn't care about her point of view because he's already made up his mind.

In reality, this couldn't be further from the truth. A man needs more information to change his mind. He may be singularly focused on results, but he'll be open to ideas that can improve his effectiveness or efficiency in attaining his goals. Men don't appreciate that women are often looking to improve a situation and are actually being supportive by questioning men's ideas and actions.

THE PERSONAL SIDE OF LIFE: "BRINGING WORK HOME"

"I'm home. Anyone home?" Sylvia calls out as she walks through the foyer.

"Up here, Mom," her son and daughter respond in unison. "I'm doing homework."

Sylvia puts her briefcase on the island and immediately starts dinner. "We'll eat in an hour," she yells at the ceiling. She can hear Tom's car pull into the driveway and wonders about his day and if he is happy in his new position. The stress of being downsized and having to accept an entry-level position in another company has shaken Tom's confidence in himself and his ability to provide for his family. It has also put a strain on his relationship with Sylvia.

"I'm home!" he calls out from the front door. "How was your day?" he asks Sylvia with a quick peck on her cheek, then walks into the family room and flips on the news. He passively stares at the television, not quite connecting yet with the images on the screen. Something catches his attention and he slowly sinks into the couch.

Sylvia runs down the list of what's racing through her mind: "I saw Dad today. I wish he would move in with us, Tom. We need to get tickets for Mark's performance next week. Do you still want to go? Before I forget, your brothers want to come over this weekend to play cards, are you still up for that? Oh, and Susie has a chemistry test tomorrow. Can you help her after dinner?"

Tom thinks quietly to himself, "All I need is a few minutes to recharge my batteries. I'll help Susie with her chemistry after dinner." He stares back at the screen and eventually yells back in the general direction of the kitchen, "What? Let's worry about those things later."

Sylvia's feelings of being ignored increase as each of her questions lands flat with no response. "Why can't he sit in the kitchen here and talk with me for a little while? That's all I want."

What happens between Sylvia and Tom demonstrates friction points that are common between so many couples today. Men and women have always had challenges in their relationships, but with the added stress of lives and careers in perpetual and unpredictable motion, relational challenges have become increasingly pronounced.

One of the foundational differences between men and women is how each gender copes with stress. Men become focused and withdrawn while women tend to become overwhelmed and emotionally involved. At these times, a man's natural ways of reducing stress are different from a woman's. He needs to disengage and forget his problems while she needs to engage and talk through hers.

Women generally don't understand how men cope with stress. They expect men to open up and talk about their problems as women do, and when a man withdraws instead of engaging, the woman tends to become upset and resentful and feelings of being ignored and excluded well up.

Men generally have little awareness of how distant they become when they withdraw into themselves. Without understanding the validity of her reactions to his disengagement, a man becomes argumentative for being misunderstood and will commonly defend himself, causing greater friction and creating greater distance.

A gender-intelligent man will realize that his partner has to communicate and share in order to reduce her stress. He would let his wife know that all he needs is 30 minutes of downtime, and after that, he'll be of more value to her. A gender-intelligent man would realize that if he tells her this, she'll tend not to feel neglected. A gender-intelligent woman will understand that her husband wants to help her but has to help himself first by coming to terms with his own issues.

When we lack gender intelligence, we lack certainty in ourselves, and we harbor anger, resentment, and mistrust of others. The challenge facing couples today is to become more aware of each other's needs and expectations, to realize that they are not the same but different, and to uncover and value the hidden complement in those differences.

FIVE

DO MEN HAVE TO WALK ON EGGSHELLS WITH WOMEN?

Women say: "No, they have it easy."
Men say: "Yes, we have our challenges there."

THE PHRASE "WALKING ON EGGSHELLS" DESCRIBES THE WAY A person approaches a sensitive topic or uncertain outcome while trying not to hurt or offend the other person's feelings. It's based on the idea that eggshells are easily broken and require delicate handling, just the approach needed to manage a conflict—exceptional care and personal restraint.

Men often find themselves walking on eggshells with women in the workplace, an apprehensive and hesitant feeling that can potentially surface any time men interact with women. Examples of situations that men say they feel most uncomfortable in and take extra care not to offend and provoke an emotional reaction include:

- Bringing up certain topics that may raise too many questions and delay decisions.
- Giving feedback during performance reviews.

- Careless language, including sexual innuendo, off-color jokes, and profanity.
- Opening doors, holding elevators, buying lunch, or offering to carry heavy packages.

GENDER FACTS[1]

- 79 percent of men feel they have to be careful and indirect when providing women critical and timely feedback.
- 82 percent of women say they want to receive direct feedback from men.

Women don't believe that men need to walk on eggshells around them. They wish that men didn't feel that way and are often surprised that it occurs to the degree that it does. Nevertheless, in our workshops and seminars, men will often claim that they have a history of "saying the wrong thing," an awkwardness that many men confess dates back to their adolescence. They'll also admit that their sense of caution is often a reaction to past situations and experiences, even if it was only an isolated incident, when something they said or did caused a woman to react negatively.

"SHOULD I HELP OR NOT?"

A man boards a plane, stows his luggage, and takes his aisle seat. He's a frequent flyer, so he's one of the first to board. He sits there reading an article and occasionally looks up to watch people board, put their luggage away, and take their seats.

A woman walks down the aisle toward him and stops two rows ahead. She looks at the overhead space and then looks down at her heavy piece of luggage. "I hate this part," she thinks to herself. She throws her handbag and jacket onto her seat and starts to lift the suitcase.

With one eye on his article and the other watching her, he immediately starts to weigh the situation. He thinks, "Should I help or not? The last woman I offered help to said, 'No, I can do it myself!' I remember how stupid that made me feel. I probably embarrassed her too."

Uncertain how to react, he freezes in his seat, then looks down at his article and continues reading. He's a little upset with himself for not showing good manners and offering her his help. He was raised to be courteous to women.

With difficulty, she lifts then forces her bag into the overhead compartment, composes herself, and takes her seat. "I wish he would have offered to help," she thinks briefly. "He was looking right at me."

This may not seem like a big deal, but it's quite symbolic of the uncertainty that sometimes passes through a man's mind when interacting with women. When this particular example was shared by one of the men in our workshop, all the other men in the room nodded knowingly—as if they've been there before and knew the feeling.

EGGSHELLS IN THE WORKPLACE

Men want to bring their best, authentic selves to work and find the most favorable ways of working with women, whether they are subordinates, peers, or supervisors. Yet men say they often feel they can't express their ideas or be their natural, casual selves without the fear of inadvertently saying or doing something that may upset a woman and prompt an undesirable emotional reaction.

Walking on eggshells around women in the workplace is not beneficial for men; it detracts from their self-confidence, personal performance, and job satisfaction. More importantly, it's not advantageous for women. A man will tend to minimize interacting with a woman he feels uneasy or uncertain around; he'll avoid topics that may raise too many questions, derail an agenda, or slow down progress. And he'll withhold candid feedback during performance appraisals and one-on-one coaching with women.

In workshops, men often admit they are more comfortable interacting with other men, especially when the other person is a stranger. A man doesn't have to think about what he's going to say around another man, whether giving critical feedback, using occasional profanity, or telling an indelicate joke.

Men say that a man's reactions are more predictable than a woman's, primarily because men tend to act more like one another than women do. Men typically have one mode of operation in the way they engage the world around them—they tend to think and act sequentially and unemotionally. They'll either solve problems or ignore them, assured that other men are thinking and acting the same way.

That men sense they must walk on eggshells with women in the workplace may seem a minor matter on the surface. But given the extent to which the sexes have been thrust together in business since the 1980s, men's tendency to feel uneasy and uncertain around women, even if it's occasional, can negatively affect the professional and personal success of both genders.

Women know they need inclusion and interaction in order to perform their jobs well and advance in their own careers. They want men to feel comfortable working with them, to be truthful to them, and to trust them. Men are generally aware of this and in turn want to be inclusive in their actions and genuine in their behavior. Yet they'll still tend to avoid situations with women that may prove uncomfortable, or are difficult to tactfully navigate, or have uncertain and unsettling outcomes.

EGGSHELLS IN THE CONFERENCE ROOM

Bill doubles his pace to catch Joe on his way to the meeting. "Hey Joe, just a heads up. I'd suggest not mentioning the results of the last survey during this meeting. The previous surveys had far larger sample sizes."

"What's wrong with the most recent survey?" Joe asks.

"The negatives were a couple of points higher and Janet will start in with her questions," Bill says. "This is a critical go/no-go meeting. We can't afford any delays."

"Don't worry about it, Bill. I've got it covered," Joe replies.

Fifteen minutes into the meeting, Janet asks, "Before we vote, what were the results of that last survey?"

During meetings men tend to be careful not to raise issues that could generate additional questions and potentially disrupt an agenda or delay a decision. Men don't typically ask questions such as, "What do you think?" Their motivation is to seek the shortest distance between two points and proceed along that path with singular focus and minimal interruption.

Men sometimes interpret a woman's questions as an unnecessary reaction to a minor issue, or a sign of not being committed to the success of the project, or as distrust of the intent of others. Unless a man thinks it's an important item that needs to be raised, he'll tend to ignore or undervalue additional questions.

It's the nature of women, however, to ask questions, and they like to have questions asked of them. It tends to give a woman a feeling of inclusion and a sense of partnership in the discovery process. They prefer to explore all sides of an issue when problem solving and before making decisions. In addition to being collaborative and eclectic in their thinking, a woman's tendency is to ask questions to demonstrate care and concern. Bringing up issues that she feels may become potential problems is her way of showing loyalty and commitment. It's a natural reaction that women have and one of their best contributions that men often and mistakenly disregard.

EGGSHELLS AT EVALUATIONS

After the performance appraisal, the manager walks into the human resources office and knocks on his HR representative's door. "It didn't

go well at all. She got very upset when I became critical of her performance over the past year. I didn't know what to do."

"Was she crying?" the HR representative asks.

"Yes," the manager replies. "Look, she dropped the ball twice this
year and we lost a client. She's a good employee, dedicated too. I want
her on my team, but I had to explain what went wrong before I could
begin to help her correct her errors."

"What did you do when she cried?" the HR representative inquires.

"To be honest, I guess I freaked out inside and then I froze. I told
her to compose herself and then ended the meeting. What should I
have done?" the manager asks.

"You should have acknowledged her feelings, told her you valued
her as an employee, and that you wanted to help her do better. Then
you should have told her what you expected of her in the future."

The manager is confused. "But she was all emotional."

"Women handle emotion differently than men do," the HR person says. "You thought her emotion was anger or fear, but it was most
likely passion for her work. Your first reaction should not be fear or
discomfort in the presence of a woman's emotional outburst."

A male supervisor will tend to hold back or soft-pedal criticism to a
woman during her performance review out of concern that if he is too
direct with his feedback or too negative in his evaluation of her, he may
upset her and provoke an emotional reaction.

In workshops, men will say that their apprehension is based on
past experience, and their uncertainty tends to prevent them from
getting to the issue with women, from providing honest evaluations,
and from offering constructive coaching. All of this hinders a woman's
chances for self-improvement and career advancement.

Men tend to be more comfortable in giving direct feedback to
other men, primarily because men's reactions are more predictable.
Male executives tend to find it much easier to coach and mentor a male

subordinate and to be critical of his performance without fear that the subordinate may take it personally.

EGGSHELLS AFTER WORK

The meeting ends and the two women clients begin to pack their briefcases as one says to the other, "So what do you want to do for dinner? Our flight doesn't leave until tomorrow morning."

Dennis, one of the three men in the conference room says, "I know a place nearby that serves great steaks. Why don't you be our guests?"

The women look at each other. They were thinking of lighter fare for dinner and a shorter evening, but together say, "Sure."

John's heart sinks. He knows what Dennis is like after a couple of drinks and doesn't want to be a part of this at all, but the women represent an important client. He can't bow out. Even worse, he can't let Dennis be alone with them. Gordon, the third man, doesn't know Dennis all that well. "Maybe he can help me navigate the evening," John thinks to himself. "I'm afraid that this is going to go south real fast!"

John is right. Dennis has two martinis before dinner, insults the server more than once, and tells a joke that can only be interpreted by the two women as being purely sexist. Dennis orders another drink with dinner and starts talking loudly and coarsely with Gordon about a film he saw last evening.

John tries his best to distract the women during dinner by asking them questions about their hometown. The women can sense John's anxiety and appreciate his efforts. Yet, they can't help but stare at Dennis in total disbelief.

The next morning the women are having breakfast before their taxi ride to the airport. "What a jerk," one says to the other. "I don't want that Dennis character anywhere near our conference next month,

and I don't want him anywhere near our CEO. She'll cancel the con-
tract with this supplier in a split second if she meets him."

Casual lunches, drinks after work, or business social events are instances where men can forget about their problems at work, relax their
conversation, and joke around. But they can't always be themselves
when women are present. A man will tend to worry about a woman in
the group misinterpreting something he may say or finding his behavior unpleasant, particularly if the behavior borders on being offensive.
For this reason, men may hesitate to ask a woman to lunch or include
women in business social events.

Many times the boundaries of decorum are not always clear, and
different women have different thresholds. All it takes is for a man
to make one unintentional comment and he could find himself in
an untenable situation. The risk of a sexual harassment charge for an
unthinking, off-color joke or sexual remark, especially after a drink
or two, is very high, and what was once a refuge for a man from the
problems of the day is now just another setting where he has to be on
guard and practice self-restraint.

In chapter one, we noted that of the roughly 12,000 sexual harassment complaints levied against men in the United States every year for
the past ten years, about half are dismissed with "no reasonable cause."[2]
Nevertheless, whether upheld, thrown out, or even brought to court
in the first place, the charge of harassment becomes a matter of record
and is enough to derail a man's career as well as negatively impacting
the reputation and position of the woman bringing suit.

Not all men worry about their own behavior around women and
often enjoy sharing a meal or drinks after work with a woman. A gender-
intelligent man feels comfortable with woman colleagues. He knows it
takes very little energy to be considerate of the women around him, and
the benefit and enjoyment of mixed company is well worth the effort.
More often than not, a man may be more uncomfortable with and try
his best to avoid a male friend who lacks that consideration.

THE DOWNSIDE FOR MEN

Men's avoidance, cautiousness, and uncertainty tend to work against a woman's sense of inclusion and her opportunities for advancement. But walking on eggshells with women is a drawback for men as well. Men want to find the best ways of working with the women in their office or on their teams, but their fear of upsetting someone's feelings by saying or doing the wrong thing can cause hesitation and uneasiness, and this tends to create a restrained, noncollaborative, and unproductive working environment.

Men can't be at their best and work effectively with women if they're unsure of themselves around women and unsure of the reactions of women around them. If his apprehensions negatively affect his ability to lead mixed teams, collaborate with female peers, or support a woman supervisor, a man's own chances for advancement may also be jeopardized.

WHY MEN ARE APPREHENSIVE

Though the social customs and cultural norms for how men and women interact vary globally, we find that many of the apprehensions men feel around women are common and most often surface for the same reasons: changing social values—particularly in the rules of civility—and the instinctual tendencies of men and women.

CHANGING SOCIAL VALUES

The women's movement for equal rights in the workplace that accelerated in the 1960s motivated a tidal wave of women seeking advanced college degrees and careers since the 1970s and 1980s. Social values tend to change from generation to generation, but within a single generation, men and women found themselves competing in the workplace for higher positions and working in unfamiliar relationships that often resulted in inauthentic behaviors—all of which left both genders feeling somewhat apprehensive and confused.

The underlying, motivational theme of equality of the sexes grew to mean that women were the same as men, that they could do the same work, apply the same thought processes and behaviors, and achieve the same results. The belief was that the differences between men and women, aside from appearance and reproductive capabilities, were the result of learned behaviors that could be unlearned. The catchphrase "Anything you can do, I can do better," appropriated from a song composed by Irving Berlin for the 1946 musical *Annie Get Your Gun*, motivated many women to believe that they could behave like men and get the same or even better results.

"BULLY BROADS" OF SILICON VALLEY

Silicon Valley during the dot-com boom of the late 1990s and early 2000s was the place of choice for young women with graduate and postgraduate degrees in management, technology, and engineering. Many became accomplished leaders in the new and growing high-tech sector and worked hard against many odds to advance in their careers.

In order to lead teams and to negotiate with vendors and partners, all of whom were primarily men, many women executives went through assertiveness training courses. The intent was to teach women in leadership positions to stand up for their rights while respecting the rights of others, and to express their own opinions, needs, and feelings without hurting the feelings of others. The goal was to teach women how to disagree without being disagreeable.

Most all of the training programs offered to women at the time were (and in many instances, still are) based on male models of behavior. Women executives were taught to solve problems sequentially and without emotion, to make quick and confident unilateral decisions, and to be task-driven and goal-oriented. Lacking appropriate female gender models that exemplified just how to be assertive, women became tough, forceful, and persistent by emulating the behavior of men in leadership positions.

Assertiveness became aggression, and the term "bully broad" surfaced to describe these forceful, uncompromising women leaders. Intelligent, aspiring young women were suddenly failing in their executive careers. A program to "take the bully out of the broad," including 360-degree assessments by subordinates, peers, and supervisors, revealed that virtually every one of the women executives who participated in assertiveness training programs scored high on many of the negative traits commonly associated with aggressive behavior: abruptness, criticism, intimidation, irritability, and control.[3]

Men typically don't know how to supervise, work with, or report to assertive women who act aggressively. Such behavior tends to confuse and suppress men and, as a result, men will commonly do their best to avoid the interactions. But if a man must work with an aggressive woman, he will do so as carefully as possible so as not to be misunderstood.

During a breakout session in our workshops, men and women are asked to list their challenges in working with the other gender. It's one of the most revealing segments of our sessions as it encourages a deeper level of participation. In one session, a male leader named Eric couldn't hold back.

"She's no longer here, but my biggest challenge was working with Susanna. She was a female bully!" All the men and women in the room agreed and started quietly exchanging stories.

When asked to describe what they meant by "bully," the men spoke up first:

- "Susanna intimidated people during meetings and put them on the spot to show how tough she was and to win the favor of the department head."

- "She would bark out orders while you stood there in her office. She would talk loudly so everyone in the hallway could hear her."
- "She would take a contrarian position on everything, always playing devil's advocate."
- "She tried to control every project and was the last to leave the office every night."

The women had something to say about Susanna's aggressiveness as well:

- "You couldn't show any weakness or doubt around her."
- "Her way of dressing like the men in the office was to always wear black. She didn't have much time for women who showed their femininity. She made you feel weak and ineffective."
- "I could never trust her. She would smile but you knew she wasn't genuine."

One woman who worked with Susanna more often than anyone else in the room summed it up for the group this way—"It was really sad. She ate lunch alone in her office and never in the cafeteria with others. She was intimidating and caustic, and she didn't have to be. She was smart and very creative. She took everything as a personal challenge. No one knew where they stood with her. The department head liked the fact that she kicked butt and got things done, but a couple of very valuable people quit because of her. I think that's why the company let her go in the end."

Behavioral models for men don't work as well when applied to women, primarily because men and women are instinctively inclined and culturally encouraged to think and behave differently. A man can generally be assertive and justify what he wants without having it based on a personal displeasure or for emotional reasons. Men tend to externalize and detach from issues in order to find solutions and feel no need to justify their assertions. Women may interpret a man's assertiveness as aggression, but other men will assume that he's simply proclaiming his desire "to get the job done."

Women tend to internalize and personalize issues. As a result, a woman's tendency will be to defend her expectations by expressing dissatisfaction and emotional discomfort. By associating her needs with a personal problem, a woman will also tend to express her assertions or demands with blame and criticism, drawing the issue inward instead of directing it externally toward getting the job done.

MODERN RULES OF CIVILITY

As children in the 1950s and 1960s, boys were instructed to be helpful to girls and women: to pull out their chairs, open doors, and lift heavy things. On dates, young men knew to pick up the check—and to do so without hesitation. They learned the rules of proper etiquette and grew to emulate the good manners that their fathers showed their mothers and other women. Movies and books were instructional for boys as they portrayed and reinforced gentlemanly behavior.

So much has changed in just one generation! Since the 1970s, there has been an upheaval of sorts in the rules of civility. Men are unsure nowadays how to be respectful or courteous to women in the workplace. They're uncertain what the rules are, and what's more confusing is that the rules and expectations can vary from one woman to the next.

Many men are concerned that their attempts to be helpful to women might be viewed as sexist for implying that she is incapable and in need of help. Complicating matters further for a woman is that if she asks for help or accepts help from a man, she may appear weak and needy.

It doesn't matter that the majority of women will often accept a man's offer to help, and it's so rare that women will object, but men are, nevertheless, still uncertain. All it takes is once or twice for a man to offer assistance and receive a negative reaction to believe that the next woman in a similar situation might respond the same disapproving way.

In today's workplace, a man will rarely compliment a woman on her appearance. It's a man's inclination to notice and admire a woman, but men are fearful of the reaction. They don't really see the harm in it, but in a business setting, complimenting a woman on her looks may not make her feel appreciated for her competence and contribution. *His* fear is that he'll forget, slip up, and say something that will be misinterpreted or not appreciated.

These shifts in social mores and cultural norms since the 1970s and 1980s bring greater clarity as to why men tend to walk on eggshells around women in the workplace. Men and women thrust together into unfamiliar roles and expected to show the same behaviors have created an environment in which both genders are prone to feeling ill at ease and confused in each other's presence. These shifts also underscore the fundamental differences in how men and women typically cope with stress, and more importantly, how they respond to each other's reactions during emotionally charged moments.

Men and women are not bringing their authentic selves to work when they lack comfort with the other gender and are not free to express themselves. We find that this feeling of uneasiness is the same for men and women all over the world, though to varying degrees. The more deep-rooted the traditional roles of men and women are in different cultures, the more difficult it is for men to work alongside women and for women to feel included and valued.

CULTURES CLINGING TO TRADITION

Every business quarter, Isabella leaves her office in Milan, Italy, to spend a week at her investment company's headquarters in Tokyo,

THE SCIENCE SIDE

Two large limbic system structures, the amygdala and hippocampus, play important roles in memory, emotions, and coping with stress.

The hippocampus is larger in women than in men, which explains why women are usually better at expressing emotions and recalling intricate physical details. It also explains why women benefit so much from talking about their problems. Women's brains are wired in such a way that they can access and freely express their emotions, all of which helps women cope with stress.[4]

Under moderate stress, women will have greater blood flow to the hippocampus,[5] while only under extreme stress will a man experience greater blood flow to his limbic system—though primarily to his amygdala, where he will process his emotions and either deal with the stressful problem, if he's able to, or ignore it.[6]

Even under moderate stress, a woman will tend to speak with an emotional voice, as her thoughts become flooded with past memories. A man will commonly misinterpret her reaction as extreme and assume she is feeling powerless to solve an overwhelming issue. He reasons that if *he* were having that level of an emotional reaction, he would need to talk through his problem with someone as well.

A woman's emotional reaction also causes a man to be cautious in saying or doing the wrong thing around women out of fear of eliciting what he believes will be an extreme emotional response. If he doesn't understand her problem or can't solve it, he'll tend to try to avoid saying or doing anything that may create a similar reaction in the future either with her or possibly other women.

His solution in dealing with the issue will be to decrease interaction and forget the incident, especially if the emotional response is blaming or critical of his behavior. Avoiding and forgetting stressful issues are central to the male paradigm of thinking, reacting, and reducing stress.

Japan, to review long-term assets, assess major investments, and make plans for the balance of the year.

During her five years with the company, Isabella has been very successful in securing profitable investments throughout Europe and was recently promoted to regional vice president because of her success. This was a unique achievement for a woman working for a Japanese company, seeing as how Japanese corporations are far below the global average of percent of women in senior executive positions.[7]

Regardless of her performance and title, Isabella has never been invited to attend a business social event during any of her 20 or so weeklong visits to Tokyo. Spending evenings in her hotel room on the busy Shibuya Crossing only punctuates her sense of aloneness and reminds her that she'll never truly be a part of the company's executive team. Because of this feeling of exclusion, Isabella is now contemplating leaving the organization.

I told Isabella that she would be making a huge mistake by quitting. Not being invited to business social events while in Japan has nothing to do with her as an individual; it's just a reality of the Japanese male culture. Japanese men are customarily uneasy having female colleagues attend their events. Though Japan is a very advanced country in business, science, and technology, much of its culture still clings to the traditional roles of men and women. This is becoming an increasingly challenging issue in Japan, for the participation of Japanese women in business is rapidly changing as a matter of economic necessity and a dire need for talent.

Greater gender intelligence will need to accompany this cultural transformation. Understanding and accepting the differences between men and women will help Japanese men become more at ease being around women colleagues in business and informal settings.

Gender intelligence will also help Isabella learn not to take their exclusion of her personally and will help her understand that cultures with steadfast traditions present the greatest challenges to men and women working openly and authentically together.

TAKING STEPS TOWARD EACH OTHER

Men walking on eggshells with women is clearly detrimental to both genders. It prevents men and women from bringing their authentic selves to work, from being open and honest in their thoughts and actions, and from building trusting relationships that can result in greater personal happiness and professional success.

The only way to achieve a higher level of personal authenticity and trust is for both men and women to take steps toward understanding and valuing each other and not expecting the other gender to make all the effort.

At the end of our workshops, we ask men and women how they would solve their workplace challenges—in this instance, how men and women might resolve men's feelings about walking on eggshells around women:

- "I adapt my language and behavior to make women feel welcome and comfortable in my presence. I certainly don't joke with women the way I joke or tease with the guys. And I'm more considerate when there are women in the room about topics that may alienate."
- "I understand and accept men's behavior and tend not to take unthinking or impulsive comments personally. I realize that men often read women's emotions incorrectly and are not inclined to remember or discuss past experiences as powerfully and expressively as women do."
- "I'm not worried about steering clear of issues that may raise questions. I know that a woman will ask questions to support,

include, and feel included, and not to derail or express doubt about a project. I realize that bringing in a variety of viewpoints will take a little longer to form a decision, but will typically produce a better outcome."

- "I've gotten better at framing my conversations with men by putting more determination behind my ideas and communicate clearly and directly with men. I frame my conversation in ways that men can understand and want to collaborate with me."

THE PERSONAL SIDE OF LIFE: PLAYING IT SAFE

Karl stepped out of his car, and as the valet drove off, he stood in the parking lot for a moment peering into the restaurant, knowing that Gretchen was already there. She was wearing something red so he could easily spot her. Karl had not yet met Gretchen, but he had spoken with her once on the phone. She suggested meeting at this restaurant after work—an arrangement convenient for both of them. "She sounded interesting and interested," he thought to himself. "I'm going to play it safe this time."

The young woman in the red dress turned around and smiled at Karl. Her eyes sparkled. "You must be Gretchen. My name is Karl." He shook her hand and held it for a moment.

"Nice to meet you Karl. Jodi has told me so many things about you. I'm happy to finally meet you."

As Karl followed the maître d' and Gretchen to their table, he could sense his uneasiness building. He was fearful of saying or doing something that might turn Gretchen off, just as his comments had on his last two dates. One woman seemed to take offense at most all of his jokes and sarcastic remarks, and the other seemed to resent his fixed opinions on social matters. "I'm not going to make those mistakes again," he reflected. "I'm playing it safe and right down the middle. No funny or controversial stuff tonight."

Throughout dinner, Karl thought he was acting on his best behavior by not coming across as a comedian or expressing his personal feelings. He was also careful not to ask Gretchen her opinion about anything because he would then feel compelled to share his thoughts, causing him to slip up and say something stupid again. The outcome was a dry and formal evening, a guarded encounter that resembled more of a job interview than a fun and entertaining date with an interesting and attractive woman.

As the evening droned on, Gretchen grew increasingly bored and disappointed. She resented having to waste her time with someone so neutral, so unsure of himself, and so obviously uninterested in her. "Karl's personality was nothing like what Jodi had described. Jodi said that he was fun and witty." Gretchen could only assume that Karl simply wasn't interested in her.

If Karl had greater gender intelligence, he would have realized that playing it safe and not being his true self would potentially create two problems: he would fail to show interest in his date, and he would suppress and misrepresent his true self to her—something Gretchen clearly wanted to see.

Karl would realize that by being himself, by being attentive to his language, and by being balanced in asking questions and sharing information about himself, he could bring out the best in Gretchen and show his best side.

If Gretchen had greater gender intelligence, she would have realized that Karl was walking on eggshells with her, not because he didn't find interest in her, but for the opposite reason—because he was quite interested but didn't want to fail with her. When she found his conversation guarded, she could have put him at ease by saying something thought provoking or funny to show that she was a woman who preferred to be with a man who had personality and wasn't afraid to be his authentic self with her.

SIX

DO WOMEN ASK TOO MANY QUESTIONS?

Women say: "Is there a problem?"
Men say: "Indeed they do."

WHEN WE EXPLORE THE CHALLENGES MEN AND WOMEN FACE in working with each other, men often state that women tend to ask too many questions. Some men even say it's a major problem especially during meetings in which they believe women's questions tend to slow down progress on action items and delay decision making.

Women generally acknowledge that they do ask more questions than men, but that their questions are their best contribution, intended to stimulate an exchange of ideas, discover what's important, and arrive at a best possible outcome.

What's unfortunate is that this question should even have to be asked. We have, for so long, stereotyped women as "always asking too many questions" to the point where today it seems that corporate cultures are more involved in suppressing the inclination instead of recognizing its incredible strength. The challenge for men is not to view women's questions as an impulse that needs to be tolerated, or minimized, or even avoided by navigating around issues, but to consider it a valuable instinct and complementary contribution, balancing a man's inclination to move (sometimes too) quickly toward a solution.

The challenge for women is not in asking fewer questions, but in understanding why men tend to believe women ask too many, and in discovering how to frame their questions in ways that communicate better with men.

GENDER FACTS[1]

- 72 percent of men state that women ask too many questions.
- 80 percent of women say they prefer to ask questions even when they know the answer.

"DOES ANYONE HAVE ANY QUESTIONS?"

"I do! How long before we see the results of the new product test?"

"Two weeks, Susan. I'll e-mail each of you the stats as soon as I receive them."

"But our regional sales managers are flying in next week for training."

"It's the best the vendor can do. The product has to be in test market long enough to validate the design. There's a number of other things I'd like to cover before this meeting is over, so if we can please move through the agenda."

"I'm still uncomfortable with this waiting period. Why didn't we let the vendor know we needed results sooner? Why do we have to wait two weeks?"

The team leader gets increasingly frustrated. "We interviewed three vendors before settling on the one we're using. Two weeks is the fastest response time we can hope for."

"Does sales support know about this delay? They're already preparing collateral and training modules for the sales managers' arrival next week and everything is based on the current design."

WHY WOMEN ASK MORE QUESTIONS THAN MEN

There are many reasons women tend to ask more questions than men—reasons that extend beyond a woman's need for information or knowledge, and therefore beyond most men's frame of reference. In our workshops, we often find that women ask questions aimed at four different purposes: to build consensus, to show concern for a project or for others, to offer feedback, and to ask for support.

Men typically don't ask as many questions. Men aren't as prone to building consensus and tend to think and process their ideas alone, even when they're working with others. They're more inclined to announce their opinions, be more direct in their requests and when offering feedback, and seldom ask for support unless they're overwhelmed with a problem and unable to solve it themselves.

"WHAT DO YOU THINK?"

Stephanie receives an e-mail with attachments from her web designer. She studies the attachments and is quite disappointed with the layout. She forwards the e-mail to Edward and Nina, her direct reports, noting, "I just received the creative for the new website. What do you think?"

Edward studies the attachments and makes a list of what he likes and dislikes and shoots an e-mail back to Stephanie and Nina: "I liked the graphics but disliked the color scheme, page layouts, and site map. My bottom line is that I don't like the creative overall and suggest the designer take a completely different approach to this."

Nina studies the attachments as well, makes a list of her likes and dislikes, and sends a reply saying, "Overall, the design has its strengths. Did you like the graphics?"

In this exchange the women asked questions to build consensus. Their questions are intended to draw out another person's thoughts first, before sharing their own opinions. Women tend to explore all sides of an issue before making a decision. By asking, "What do you think?" a woman is not necessarily seeking final thoughts or a solution, but is creating or sustaining a conversation, or strengthening a relationship. In addition to asking questions, a woman likes to have questions asked of her, because they make her feel included and they indicate an interest and an appreciation for her ideas.

"ARE YOU SURE THAT'S THE BEST SOLUTION?"

Women express their care and concern through questions. Raising issues is a woman's way of showing her commitment and loyalty. Women tend to notice things and recall past events in greater detail than men. Add to this an inclination to interconnect those past events and a woman usually will feel a deeper sense of consequence, which in turn compels her to question a decision. As in this situation—

The CEO convenes his executive team. "I've looked over the numbers and I think we should discontinue the product line. It's barely profitable and it's not a strategic priority going forward. This is a big decision for our company, but I can't see us maintaining four product lines with this one barely making us money. Everything has to pull its weight around here."

The chief financial officer confirms the CEO's observations. "The profit margin on this line is lower than that of our three other lines, and we've been barely breaking even on it for the past two years. I think it's going to continue to slide. If we want to remain viable and grow, we need to trim our sails!"

One of the two women on the executive team doesn't have the facts to support her opinion, but she just made a connection that, she worries, the others may have missed. Although she'd be sticking her neck out to voice her concern, it's either now or never. "Are you sure that's the best solution? I mean, the product line might have the lowest margin, but our three largest retailers rely on that brand. I'm not sure what percent of our sales those three chains represent, but I'm pretty sure they're our largest customers. My concern is if we discontinue the line, we lose those retailers. And if we lose them, we could lose one or more of our top sales executives."

The CFO immediately jumped to the defense of the CEO, who was visibly nonplussed by her speculation. "We have to focus on the bottom line and we're barely breaking even on that brand. Those retailers rely on us for more than one product, and I don't see how it's going to hurt our sales force in the long run."

A woman will, at times, surface questions that a man may consider unrelated to the issue, or he'll misinterpret her questions as signs of uncertainty or a reluctance to make a hard decision. A man may even interpret her indirect questions as a personal challenge to his competency or integrity.

A man will tend to act more positively to a direct question with factual data because it comes across as being less personal, less ambiguous, and gives him a linear path of reasoning, something he can respond to and resolve. In this instance, she could have responded to the CFO with, "I feel strongly about this. Give me a couple of days to pull together the information, including getting feedback from the three retailers, before we make the decision."

"WHY IS THIS PROJECT SO FAR OFF SCHEDULE?"

Women don't often feel at ease giving direct, negative feedback, so they'll commonly express their disapproval or disagreement through a rhetorical, indirect question. Rather than specifically ask, "Why are you late on this project?" a woman might ask, "Why is this project being delayed?" to appear less aggressive and demanding.

For example—it was ten in the morning when Kerry walked into "the pit," the name the programmers gave their workspace. Three of the five programmers were there, sitting in a circle, eating breakfast sandwiches and talking.

"Where are Luke and Matt?" Kerry asked.

"They're not here yet," said one of the programmers.

"I need to meet with all five of you when they get here. I need to know why this project is so far off schedule. Would you please come to my office when everyone is in?"

Jim, her colleague, happened to be walking with her and had something to say about that exchange. "Kerry, if I may suggest something, you should have been more forceful. Asking them a question is not forceful, but stating a fact is. You should have said, 'You guys are two weeks late on this project and I need to meet with you in one hour to discuss it. Call Luke and Matt and let them know.' These guys are good programmers, but they'll only do what they're told and no more. You really have to be more direct."

Men tend to be impersonal and direct in their feedback. A man will separate himself from the issue, disconnecting from his past experiences and emotions. Detached and impartial, he becomes more at ease giving candid feedback, primarily because he's externalized the problem. A woman will often interpret his directness and assertiveness as aggressive behavior while the man believes he's being neutral and straightforward.

"WOULD YOU HAVE THE TIME TO LOOK AT THIS?"

Women don't often feel comfortable asking for support in the workplace. In certain situations, asking for support implies weakness, and women are reluctant to show vulnerability, given that some men already tend to prejudge women. A woman will tend to be more suggestive and indirect when asking for help, and when unsupported, may express her need as a frustration—a reaction a man will tend to interpret as criticism or blame.

- "I can really use another pair of eyes on this presentation. Would you have the time to look at this? I've been working on these slides all morning and I'm not sure if I'm on the right track. It's hard to get feedback with everyone so busy."

Men too can be just as reluctant to seek support, partly to avoid being viewed as weak or incompetent, and asking for help can be seen as a sign of weakness. For this reason, a man will often not ask for help and will try to solve a problem without any assistance until he discovers and admits that it may be beyond his ability to solve alone. For example, often a man's first inclination is not to ask for directions when lost.

If a man does ask for help, he won't ask for support from a position of weakness but from a position of strength. He'll frame his request directly and encourage the support of another man by making the other person feel competent and special. Let's assume it was a man working on that presentation all morning. Here's how he might have directly asked for support:

- "I finished the presentation! I think it's pretty complete but I would value your judgment. You seem to have a good mind for these things. Could you give it a once over and let me know what your thoughts are?"

HOW MEN MISINTERPRET WOMEN'S QUESTIONS

Men and women contribute differently when giving their best in the workplace. Women tend to ask questions to create an inclusive environment, to build relationships, and to express care and concern for others and for the work at hand. A man will typically not ask as many questions, and when he does, his approach will be more direct. A man can be direct without being personal, and will often not take it personally when someone is being direct with him. Approach him indirectly and he can become frustrated, confused, and even offended with questions that he may interpret as time consuming, indecisive, or personal.

SEEKING CLARIFICATION OR IMPLYING DOUBT?

In team meetings and one-on-one discussions, a woman will often demonstrate her interest and concern by asking questions to draw out the other person's thoughts and to explore all sides of a problem or opportunity. She'll ask clarifying questions to connect with others and encourage them to think through and share their points of view. When women use questions to draw a man out or to expand on his thinking, the man will often assume she's being critical or doubtful of his contribution, as in the following exchanges.

A team of five women and two men are having their standard Monday morning group meeting. Judy, the department head, has already gone around the room asking each woman on the team for their thoughts on the new corporate initiative, and each has expressed her opinion. Judy hasn't heard from the two men yet. "So Mark and Collin, we've heard from everyone else on this, what do you guys think?"

Mark and Collin look at each other for a split second, then Mark speaks first. "I don't know. I'm still processing everything." He doesn't look at Collin again because looking at Collin is body language for "it's Collin's turn to respond." He's going to let Collin handle this one on his own!

"So, Collin, what about you?" Judy asks again.

"I don't know. I haven't thought it through yet, Judy. It looks like a good idea. I'd like to give it more thought."

Seldom will a man consider drawing another man out to encourage participation and to share ideas. Part of the male code is never to put another man on the spot publicly. Just as much as women commonly ask questions and, in return, like to have questions asked of them, men don't often like to ask or be asked questions. A man assumes that if another man has something to say he'll throw his ideas into the mix, or he'll remain quiet.

A man doesn't mind being challenged as long as he senses that his words and actions are not being taken personally. When a man believes that he's being doubted, criticized, or blamed, he'll tend to take it personally and react defensively, or he'll become frustrated and go silent because he can no longer be seen as the solution to the problem.

"LET'S JUST SHELVE IT."

In one of our workshops, we learned that a new product development team had decided to cancel a new product concept even though research indicated that the product had the potential to capture a significant share of market. After a half-day of deliberations, the men on the team and their male leader acted in a very decisive way and decided to kill the product.

The women on the team didn't want to make a go/no-go decision for further product development until additional research was conducted on a very small percentage of disinterested consumers. The women wanted to know why those consumers were so against the product. The women felt that "where there's smoke, there's fire," and what might be an isolated thing could trigger a bigger issue later on.

None of the men believed the additional research was necessary, and they interpreted the women's request as a lack of confidence in the new product concept—and for some of the men, as a personal challenge to their integrity.

The women didn't want to end product development; they also thought it had potential. They felt that the percentage of consumers, although small in number, might be pointing to an issue that should be taken into consideration now.

REQUESTS OR CRITICISM?

When engaging with others, women have the capacity to notice more than men—from facial expressions, to body language, to tone of voice. It's common for a woman to intuitively pick up these messages, sense the needs of others, and automatically lend her support. For this reason, a woman often makes the mistake of believing she doesn't have to ask directly for support. She'll expect others to be as attentive as she is and react the same way she does. The reality is that men are just not as perceptive as women are.

When a woman openly gives her support but doesn't directly ask for support in return, a man's tendency is to assume she's already getting what she needs. He won't immediately offer his support, not because he's unwilling to help, but because he's most likely waiting to be asked. A man's tendency is to not offer another man unsolicited support and to deal with women similarly. If she doesn't ask for support, he's most likely not going to offer it.

She asks an indirect question	What she may really be saying	How he interprets her question
"What does it take to get things done around here?"	"I can use your support in getting this completed."	"I assume she'll ask for my help if she needs it."
"Are you okay preparing this presentation by yourself?"	"I'm here if you need me."	"I get the feeling she doesn't think I can handle it."
"I don't understand. Why hasn't the equipment arrived yet?"	"Please find out what's holding up the supplier."	"I don't know why the equipment hasn't arrived yet."
"Shouldn't we approach the client in this manner?"	"I know how to handle this, but I want your input."	"Just tell me what you want and I'll do it."
"Is that really true?"	"That amazes me."	"I get the impression you don't believe me."

Here are some examples of how a woman will indirectly make a request or ask for support, what her true intention may be, and how a man may interpret her indirect question:

BEHIND EVERY COMPLAINT IS AN UNSPOKEN REQUEST

When a woman doesn't express herself in a direct manner, it leaves room for a man to hear all kinds of messages that sound as if she's demanding, disapproving, or blaming. Rather than deal with the complaint, a man would prefer to address the request and solve the problem head on.

In each of the examples in the chart on the previous page, a woman could help a man get the right message and immediately gain his support simply by adding a non-blaming, upbeat comment before the question, or by making a clear and direct request:

- "I can use your support in completing this work."
- "I know you can handle it, but I'm here if you need me."
- "Please find out what's holding up the supplier."
- "I have a great idea, but first tell me your approach."
- "That amazes me. Is it really true?"

"I WASN'T SURE OF HER INTENT"

The chief operating officer of a global petroleum company recently asked me to help him get to the bottom of why he was on the brink of losing two very valuable employees—the president of Middle East operations and one of the company's top chemical engineers.

Anne was recently hired to head up operations in the Middle East, a position she viewed as a welcome challenge in the same industry of her father's and brother's successful careers. The region had never had a woman president before and her colleagues—all male engineers—never had a woman boss before.

During my meeting with Anne, she pinpointed the breakdown in communication to the very first meeting with her team when she asked a number of questions during the lead engineer's presentation. She thought that by asking Haitham questions during his report, he would understand her interest, but it didn't impress him that way.

"I didn't think his reaction would be so defensive," Ann recalled. "My intent was to get up to speed as quickly as possible on all the activities in the region and to build a trusting, sharing relationship with the team."

Haitham saw things differently. "I wasn't sure of her intent. I'm not used to being questioned that way in front of the other engineers. I hold a Ph.D. in chemical engineering and have been working for this company for over 20 years. I have a great record of achievement. It was clear to me that she didn't believe my requests and was insinuating that I wasn't doing my job well enough. I don't need someone watching over me and slowing down my progress. So I went to her boss and lodged my complaint."

Anne was clearly upset that Haitham misinterpreted her intentions and went over her head. When trust is lost, it's almost impossible to regain, and the loss of trust between Anne and Haitham proved devastating to the team and harmful to the company's momentum in the region.

Haitham could have shown greater gender intelligence by understanding that Anne was not criticizing him but looking to add value and build a relationship. He could have recognized this by not taking her questions personally and not reacting defensively.

Anne could have shown greater understanding as well by realizing that her attempt to draw Haitham out embarrassed him and challenged his intentions. She could have set the stage by opening with, "My door is open. If you need anything, just give me a call. I'm here to support you. In the meanwhile, I trust you to get the job done."

THE SCIENCE SIDE

Women tend to reflect on issues quite differently than men by integrating and arranging memories and emotions into more complex, web-like patterns of thought. As a result, women in contrast to men tend to weigh more variables, consider more options, and visualize a wider array of solutions and outcomes to a problem.

How and why women perceive and judge things differently than men, and feel compelled to ask more questions as a result, is often influenced by several critical parts of the brain that are larger, more interconnected, and more active in women than in men: the anterior cingulate cortex (ACC), the prefrontal cortex (PFC), and the insula.[2]

The anterior cingulate cortex is larger in women than in men and plays a role in a wide variety of involuntary functions, such as regulating blood pressure and heart rate, as well as influencing rational cognitive functions such as anticipation, decision making, empathy, and emotion. As a result, women tend to weigh options, ruminate, and express concerns more often and in a deeper contextual setting than men.

The prefrontal cortex is the decision-making, executive center of the brain that oversees emotional information and controls the amygdala in women through consequential thinking. The PFC is not only larger in women but also develops faster in young girls than in young boys. This difference, combined with the fact that women have far less testosterone and far more estrogen flowing through their brains, influences women to make fewer impulsive decisions than men and to search for solutions to conflict before taking immediate action.[3]

The insula is, on average, twice as large in the female brain than in the male brain and helps a woman translate physical sensations and thoughts in the subconscious mind into conscious thoughts flooded with memories and emotions. This ability to draw on past memories and bring them into the present prevents a woman from acting hastily and taking unnecessary risk. In conjunction with the ACC and PFC, the insula helps a woman anticipate what something may feel like before it actually happens, making a "woman's intuition" a very real biological difference.

Given the size and interconnectedness of these brain centers, women are more inclined to think and reflect in webs of factors. Men, on the other hand, tend to focus their attention on one thought at a time, compartmentalize relevant information, discard what they may consider extraneous or irrelevant data, and analyze information along a narrow, linear path.

Couple this difference in brain structure with varying hormonal levels and the difference in thinking between women and men becomes even more accentuated. A man's higher levels of testosterone compel him to seek immediate solutions and take quick action, while a woman's lower levels of this hormone and higher levels of estrogen may contribute to her broader, more contextual, more long-term view of things.[4]

A woman's natural ability for interconnected, consequential thinking is a strength that men tend to undervalue and misinterpret as expressions of uncertainty and insecurity. A man's instant ability to scan his environment for reason and logic and take immediate action is a strength that women tend to misinterpret as being dismissive, uncaring, and risk inclined.

The reality is that men's and women's natural orientations are perfectly complementary ways of thinking and reasoning. Neither men nor women alone have all the answers, but when working together, they can discover that their natural differences can produce exponentially better results.

ASKING QUESTIONS AND LISTENING

Over the years, we've conducted many gender intelligence workshops with investment firms on Wall Street. One of our greatest insights in this industry actually came the day after a workshop with Jane, the chief financial officer of one of the largest investment banking firms in New York. She participated in the workshop, then agreed to a one-on-one discussion the following morning.

Jane had been promoted to CFO in 2010, two years after the banking crisis of 2008, and she had a number of observations on the value of gender balance in investment banking. She believed that a better blend of men and women in decision making could have prevented many of the mistakes that led up to the financial crisis.

"Traditionally, the CFO primarily focused on financial reports, compliance, treasury, tax, and corporate finance. What we're seeing now is that CFOs are far more involved in both strategy and operations.

Asking questions and listening are two of the most important things we can do as financial leaders. In addition to being up to speed on anything that is going on finance-wise, I have to understand what's going on in the business. I have to ask good questions and then listen carefully in order to synthesize, spot trends, and communicate to key constituencies including our investors, board of directors, key customers, and Wall Street analysts.

"This is a good thing, because it connects the dots across the organization and helps to integrate the strategy and operations with financial forecasts and results. Since 2008, companies have become far more careful about investments. There is less of a propensity to take risks without informed and rigorous investigation and analysis.

"What I don't want is for my department to be a compliance function to the rest of the business. That 'blind obedience' tends to get us in financial trouble, and we've seen that in the past with risky investments. I want our finance people to work with their business sponsors and question their decisions. We're there to help the business grow profitably, but in a compliant way."

Jane is on the leading edge of a growing trend in investment banking. According to recent studies, a few more women investment bankers could have prevented the banking crisis and resulting recession. Women, often criticized for their risk-aversive tendencies, are now being told it is exactly those tendencies that could have prevented quite a lot of fiscal damage with a better balance of risk-taking men and risk-averse women in the industry.

These studies show that women are more than twice as likely to be cautious, questioning, and prudent, while men are more than twice as likely to be adventurous, overly confident, and carefree in their investment decisions. What is very unexpected is the strength of those differences.[5] Overconfidence causes men to trade stocks 45 percent more often than women, thus lowering their net portfolio returns by 2.65 percent per year (compared with 1.72 percent lower returns for women traders).

These studies also show a link between profit and gender. Financial companies with several high-ranking women at either officer or director levels tend to have higher earnings per share, higher return on equity, and higher stock prices than competitors with few or no senior women. Women select a return target and then seek to lower risk while men select a risk target and then seek to maximize potential gain. Women tend to see risk in a contextual framework and select investments that take into account consequential effects such as social value, long-term impact, and client needs. Men, on the other hand, tend to approach investing sequentially and separately, and tend not to consider social concerns as much as women do when they look for the highest gain. Generally, women are better investors because they are better observers, questioners, and listeners.

The bottom line is that companies that have a blend of both approaches to risk assessment realize better financial results overall compared to companies that employ only male investors. Companies that have not yet learned to complement the different behaviors and risk tolerances of men and women tend not to be as successful.

THE PERSONAL SIDE OF LIFE: DATING AND PARENTING

Without an understanding of women's customs and manners, a man may think he's putting his best foot forward on a first date and unknowingly turn his companion off. As long as she's asking him questions, he'll continue to talk about himself. He assumes this is what she expects, and he's more than happy to oblige.

Men don't typically share the same manners as women. Women demonstrate consideration and caring for others by asking questions and being careful not to dominate the conversation. When two women come together, typically one starts out by asking questions and listening with interest. Then after a short while, they'll switch roles and the first questioner-listener will tell about herself while the other woman listens and asks questions.

This alternating manner of listening and sharing is significant in a woman's communication process. It also becomes her expectation when on a date. If she shows interest in the man, she'll assume that he'll show interest in her. So she'll continue to ask questions, thinking that he'll eventually "get it" and ask her about herself. She could be waiting quite a while though. A man often doesn't understand that he's supposed to reciprocate and show his interest in her by asking her questions about herself and by listening with genuine attentiveness.

Women don't play by the same rules as men. It's not in a woman's "book of manners" to interrupt. Whether instinctually or as a result of her upbringing or culture, interrupting someone just doesn't commonly feel natural. She'll tend to ask questions first, then wait her turn to speak.

A man, on the other hand, is often comfortable with interrupting another man when in a discussion. Neither of them actually considers it an interruption. A friendly, non-personal intrusion in the middle of a sentence is something a man can often expect, and he'll just roll with it. In a way, not taking turns talking tends to make the whole process of communication much easier for men.

A man incorrectly assumes that if his date is not talking, she probably has nothing to say. Correspondingly, a woman mistakenly assumes that if he is not asking her questions, then he's probably not interested in her. The challenge for women is in knowing how and when to interrupt a man. Asking permission to interrupt with questions such as, "May I ask you a question?" or "Can I say something?" tends to show insecurity and breaks the flow of conversation. A man expects a woman simply to join in, which is what she should feel comfortable doing.

The challenge for a man is to realize that showing interest in her by asking questions, instead of trying to impress her with his own thoughts on life and his personal accomplishments, is a far more effective way of having her develop an interest in him.

Rhetorical questions are fine when you're trying to make a point in a persuasive speech, but they are counterproductive when asking for cooperation, whether in one's professional or personal life. For every rhetorical question, there is an implied message, and in parenting the implied message is often a negative, guilt- or blame-filled comment that parents would prefer not to make directly to their child. Instead, a parent will indirectly suggest his or her disappointment or dissatisfaction in a roundabout way.

Women, in particular, will use rhetorical questions to try to motivate children to be obedient. When a mother wants her child to clean up his or her room, instead of saying, "Could you please clean up your room?" she tends to impart a little shame or little guilt first through a rhetorical question, such as, "Why is this room a mess?" Other examples of rhetorical, indirect questions include:

- "When are you going to grow up?" implying the child is behaving in an immature manner.
- "How could you forget to close the garage door?" implying the child is undependable.
- "Why is the light still on and you're still up?" implying the child doesn't listen.
- "Why haven't you finished your homework?" implying the child is lazy or doesn't care.

In each of these examples, the parent is trying to encourage the child to do something by focusing on the problem, but in reality, ends up not asking the son or daughter to do anything specific. The implied request is often not even realized by the child, who will tend to stare blankly into space.

By not asking rhetorical questions before making a request, parents increase their chance of creating cooperation and getting results; otherwise children will just stop listening because the parents' requests have no apparent consequences. One of the most important skills for parents to learn, particularly mothers seeking to get results from their young sons, is not to imply displeasure or personal pain to generate a desired response, but to be direct and positive with their request.

SEVEN

DO MEN LISTEN?

Women say: "No, and it's my number one complaint!"
Men say: "What do you mean? Of course I listen."

ONE OF THE MOST STIMULATING AND INSIGHTFUL MOMENTS OF
our workshops occurs when men and women break into separate teams
and explore the challenges they face in working with the other gender.
As you would expect, the women immediately begin relating and sharing their experiences, while the men usually take a few extra minutes
to warm up before talking. They'll quietly sit there at first, with looks
of curiosity and astonishment over the instantaneous buzz of activity
at the women's tables.

What never ceases to amaze us are the similarities in the challenges
raised by women, regardless of the country, with women most often
admitting that their number one issue is that men don't listen. Men are
usually surprised when they hear this, and their predictable response

GENDER FACTS[1]

- 98 percent of men and women feel communication is important,
  though only 52 percent of women feel fully heard by men.
- 82 percent of men feel they are communicating well enough to
  women and believe they are being understood.

is, "Of course we listen!" which sparks a lively discussion that is both revealing for women and enlightening for men.

The greater insight is that men do listen, but not always in ways that communicate to a woman that she's being heard.

"WAS I SUPPOSED TO SAY SOMETHING?"

A woman manager looks up from the copier in frustration and remarks, "These things never work!" A male colleague, the only other person in the copy center—and just a few feet away from her—is completely absorbed in sorting out the slides for his presentation. He hears her and stops for a moment and thinks, "I don't know anything about copy machines. Does she want me to do something? There's another copier at the other end of the hall." He can't come up with anything to say and goes right back to organizing his slides.

She thinks he's rude for not acknowledging her and at least saying something supportive. Another woman would have said something to show understanding such as, "I know! Those things never work when you need them to." That's all the woman wanted to hear. She wasn't necessarily asking him to come over and fix the copier.

These thoughts are running through her mind while she's trying to get the machine to work. He, on the other hand, has already forgotten all about her comment and is completely absorbed in his presentation again.

In the last chapter, we learned that women often ask questions or share their observations to build partnerships, strengthen trust, or show support. A woman tends to formulate her thoughts by talking things through. This process of just letting her feelings and ideas flow freely and expressing them aloud helps her to access her memories and experiences, explore consequences, and, in the process, reduce her stress. This process is perfectly normal and quite beneficial for her, but not necessarily for him.

Men tend to silently mull over and think about things before sharing what's on their mind. Internally and quietly, they'll figure out the most correct or useful response, a process that can take several seconds, a few minutes, or even hours, and this is what's most confusing and off-putting to women. If a man doesn't have enough information to respond, or her question or comment falls outside his linear pattern of thinking, he may not say anything at all or very little. This in turn gives a woman the impression that he's not listening, isn't interested in what she's saying, or doesn't care.

One of the leading ways men sabotage their success in working with women is by not taking the time to show that they are listening and, in the process, demonstrate their concern and consideration.

Women, in turn, tend to sabotage their success in working with men by expressing irritation or resentment for a man's silence and assuming he isn't paying attention or doesn't care. As in the example above, the man in the copy center may have no clue that his coworker is offended by his silence, and to complicate matters further, he may become offended at her taking offense because he didn't say something in response.

WHEN WOMEN FEEL MEN AREN'T LISTENING

Without understanding the different ways and reasons a woman may ask a question to share what she knows or needs, or make an opening remark to stimulate conversation, or express her feelings to show support, a man will often respond inappropriately or fail to react at all.

When a woman complains that men don't listen, she may be recalling past instances in which a man failed to take notice of what she was saying, misinterpreted her intent, or undervalued her contribution. These are the most common ways that indicate to a woman that a man is not listening:

- He ignores what she's saying.
- He interrupts her in mid-thought.
- He presumes to know what she's thinking.
- He becomes easily distracted.

This is not a huge mystery for men to understand, and there are ways men can better communicate to women that they are indeed listening. There are also ways a woman can capture his attention, ensure that she's being heard, and generate the response she wants or needs to hear.

"YOU MISSED MY POINT."

When men fail to give the proper signals that they're listening, women begin to feel that their words are not getting through. A woman's sense of being excluded or dismissed—reactions explored in previous chapters—stem from men not responding in ways that a woman values and appreciates. This leads a woman to feel that she's being ignored, that what she's saying is not that important, or that *she's* not that important.

Mariana was part of a very small group of women to receive a Ph.D. in food science from the California Institute of Technology in the late 1980s. In those days, you could count the women with doctorate degrees from Caltech on one hand. Mariana was one of those early pioneers who knew exactly what she wanted to do, and she would return to Brazil with her simple but passionate dream—to develop the first and best line of health foods for dogs and cats.

For almost 20 years, Mariana served as CEO and chaired the board of directors of her small but rapidly growing company, expanding its reach to cover all of South America, then exponentially across the globe with the advent of the Internet for online ordering and distribution. Her stepping down as CEO was long overdue, so the search began for her successor.

Mariana's intent was to remain as the board's chairperson to ensure that the business would continue to reflect her personal philosophy and the corporate culture she wanted to maintain. She was very clear to her board as to what she was looking for in a CEO: "It's not just about making money; it's about supporting the emotional relationship pet owners have for their pets. That's how I want to distinguish us from our competition, and I want to ensure that my successor shares that philosophy."

Her board of directors, comprised of women and men, spent several months interviewing candidates with the intent of narrowing the field down to two from whom Marianna would make her final choice. The board was satisfied with their two finalists, in particular Robert, an industrious, visionary leader and an expert in online distribution and social media. Mariana met Robert for the first time during the final interview process and began the meeting by sharing her philosophy for the future of the company. As soon as Mariana finished her opening remarks, Robert launched into his presentation outlining his plans to take the business to the next level.

Mariana knew she needed someone with Robert's drive and experience, but her intuition told her that he would never be the company leader that she was looking for. All she wanted was for Robert to acknowledge her business philosophy during any part of his presentation, but he never gave her the indication that he understood and agreed. Though the men on the board thought he was the perfect candidate, she was not convinced, and he didn't get the job. Robert simply failed to reassure Mariana that he shared her business philosophy.

In the workplace, a man tends to be so task-oriented and singularly focused that he'll often, though unintentionally, overlook or dismiss the ideas of others, giving the impression that he's uninterested or indifferent. He may show the proper care and concern for producing the best product or providing the best service, but if he doesn't succeed in communicating that he acknowledges the ideas and needs of others around him, he may lose the trust, creativity, and commitment of those most critical to his success.

"BUT WE *ARE* ON THE TOPIC!"

One of the largest law firms in Chicago needed to find the underlying cause of why they were losing their most experienced female attorneys to a competing law firm. The law firm formed a task force of male and female partners to review the financials, determine the impact of the turnover, and get to the root cause of why the best upcoming women lawyers were leaving. A male attorney, the most senior partner with the firm, began the meeting by reviewing the statistics and assessing the financial damages.

The three women on the task force started sharing their experiences with the women who had quit the firm, looking for patterns that may have prompted their leaving. The men, on the other hand, focused on the statistics, the cost of attrition, and if the departing women had any effect on the firm's billable hours.

Two different conversations ensued—one centered on the financial impact and the other on the root cause. Finally, the senior partner, in his effort to rein the women back into the discussion the men were having said, "Ladies, ladies, can we get back to the topic at hand?" The women, quite upset at the insinuation that they were even off subject, replied in unison, "But we *are* on the topic!"

"IF I MAY JUST FINISH MY THOUGHT . . ."

Men are accustomed to interrupting each other, whether in group meetings or one-on-ones, and tend not to take it personally when it happens to them. Men collaborate to compete, even where there's nothing to compete over. They'll cut in to a conversation to toss in their opinion or build on someone else's contribution with a better idea.

It's a lot like passing a ball back and forth as players move down field to score a point. Think of the meeting as the playing field, the agenda as the playbook, and each decision made as a point scored. With every game, there are rules of engagement, and one of the principal rules in this game is that any idea tossed into play must be relevant to the topic at hand. If the interruption is off track, a man will often quickly interject to steer the discussion back on track. A man tends to believe that to achieve a goal, he must focus on the most effective and efficient means of getting there, and he'll tend to ignore or dismiss any discussion that falls out of bounds.

Interruptions are very natural to a man's way of thinking and acting but unnatural and unmannerly to women. If a man interrupts a woman to make a point or offer advice, and he's on target, the last thing he would feel is that he wasn't listening. He expects her to say, "Good point!" while all the while she may be thinking, "I'm not really looking for advice. I just wanted to think this through with you, so please let me finish."

Men love to solve problems and often feel honored to have the opportunity to help resolve an issue. Bringing a problem to a man is an open invitation for his advice. If he senses frustration or anxiety in a woman's voice, a man will tend to assume that it's his responsibility to step in and put her mind at ease.

She'll feel he isn't listening when he interrupts her in midsentence with something like, "No, no, no, here's what you should do." He thinks his quick reaction and the relevance of his solution proves he was listening. The woman may only have wanted him to lend an ear, not render a decision.

Here are some examples of how a man will cut in to get his point across, to get a discussion back on track, or to offer advice when a woman is more interested in creating dialogue, leaving her with the impression that he isn't truly listening.

What she says	What she may really be saying	How his response shows he isn't listening
"First, let me share this story with you."	"This is relevant and will help clarify my point."	"I don't see what that has to do with this."
"Maybe we should consider that outcome before we make a decision."	"Just think this through with me for a minute."	"I think we've got a good plan here already."
"May I ask a question?"	"I have a better idea."	"Let's keep moving forward and we'll cover questions later."
"I was invited to attend the session but have my doubts."	"I'm not sure if I want to attend or not."	"I think you should go to the meeting, period!"
"I'll never get it done today."	"I'll feel better if I can just talk about it for a minute with you."	"Don't worry about it. It's not that important anyway."

A woman will often talk to find her focus while a man's tendency is to focus before talking. At times, a woman will start her conversation from a whole other premise with something like, "I was talking to Stephen the other day and he got me thinking," then eventually get to the point she is trying to make. This process allows her to sort out her priorities and gain clarity on the most important issue or issues she needs to resolve in her own mind.

Women often explore issues in a broader context than men and with more thought given to the consequences of a decision: "Is this the best thing for the company?" or "Is this the best thing for the environment?"

Speaking her mind will often allow a woman to reach a place of greater understanding. The action of self-expression helps her to unfold her thoughts and understand herself better in the process. When a man breaks that flow by interrupting her thinking process and finishing her thought for her, it can be distracting and frustrating. If she's sharing her concern over accomplishing a task on time, a better response on his part would be, "What's making you feel that way?" which gives her a chance to reveal and maybe resolve the obstacles in her path.

Women tend to not interrupt other women because they don't like being interrupted themselves. A woman's tendency is to allow the other person time to think through and share what's on his or her mind. She'll encourage the conversation with, "That's interesting, tell me more." To her, building a relationship is as important as finding a solution.

Women simply don't play the same game that men do—but if a woman can understand why a man interrupts, she can encourage a man to listen and be more supportive in the long run. A man's tendency is to solve problems, but he will wait patiently and listen if that's what he's been asked to do. The best way to do this is to be very explicit by asking at the onset of a conversation, "I need your help and would like your opinion about something, but let me first give you a little background."

"HE'S SO EASILY DISTRACTED."

Susan stands at the entrance to her colleague's cubicle and says, "Peter, I think we're going to have a big problem with this new supplier. The shipment hasn't arrived yet and the client is on his way here to pick it up."

Peter stares at his computer screen and just can't seem to pull his eyes away. The screen is like a tractor beam holding his attention. He's on a deadline, and instead of looking up at her, he continues entering data into his spreadsheet and mumbles, "Uh huh."

She keeps talking, detailing the situation with the hope that he'll break away from what he's doing and focus on her problem. Peter, all the while, thinks he's listening, though in reality he's only giving her about 10 percent of his attention.

Susan, now with an irritated voice, asks, "Are you listening to me, Peter?"

Peter responds without looking up from his screen, "Yeah, I can hear you . . . a supplier problem?" He starts to become aggravated because he doesn't want to shift gears and now he's thinking, "Is what she's saying more important than this spreadsheet?" She stands there for a moment, waiting for him to acknowledge her. He eventually adds, "What were you saying?"

When a man is under stress, he'll develop tunnel vision, the tendency to focus exclusively on a single or limited goal or point of view while ignoring everything else around him. Having to take in what Susan's saying while trying to make his deadline is too distracting and stressful for Peter, but not necessarily for her. Women have a capacity to multitask and often do much better at dealing with more than one stressful issue at a time. They find it difficult to believe that men can't function the same way. As a result, Susan will conclude that "he not listening," or worse, "he's intentionally ignoring me."

Peter's inability to give Susan his full attention may have nothing to do with her, but with the manner in which she's communicating. If she is not getting right to the point, his mind will begin to drift to other things more pressing or urgent to him. Another man wouldn't take it personally and would conclude, "This guy's busy. I'll just come back later."

When a man shows himself to be distracted, either by not looking directly at a woman when she's talking with him, fidgeting with his watch, looking around the room, or checking his phone for e-mail messages, a woman tends to take it personally and conclude that he's not interested in what she's saying or that she's unimportant to him.

THE SCIENCE SIDE

While there are essentially no differences in general intelligence between the genders, there are significant differences in the brain areas where men and women reveal that intelligence. Gray matter represents information processing centers in the brain and white matter the nerve fibers that network or connect those processing centers. Studies show that women have more white matter than men do, and men have more gray matter than women; both types of brain matter are related to intellectual ability. "In general, men have more gray matter related to general intelligence than women do, and women have more white matter related to intelligence than men."[2]

This may help to explain why men tend to do better in tasks that require centralized processing, like math, while women, because of their abundance of white matter, tend to excel at integrating and assimilating information from gray-matter regions in the brain, as in language learning and alternative or consequential thinking. Nevertheless, according to the research, "these two very different neurological pathways and activity centers still result in equivalent overall performance on broad measures of cognitive ability, such as those found on intelligence tests."[3] This physical difference in each gender's brain composition is one of the reasons that helps to explain why men and women communicate so differently. A woman's brain is typically constructed to communicate and express feelings, and, since it's always busy absorbing and connecting data, is far more active than a man's. The more a woman cares about something, the more she connects it to other memories and experiences registered deep in her limbic system.

Men typically have a harder time connecting their emotions with their thoughts and articulating what they feel. A man will often not respond as quickly as a woman because he may be taking more time to process information if he is making a connection, or not respond at all if there are no associated memories and emotions stored to be recalled. Moreover, a man's language and listening centers are particularly active when he is solving a problem, but once that problem is solved, these areas of his brain are far less activated.

As an example, when a woman comes home from work, or a trip, or a visit with a friend, she may have a lot to impart from what she experienced and is eager to share how everything connects. The process of communicating and sharing actually helps increase her oxytocin levels and thereby reduces her stress. Oxytocin, a hormone connected to childbirth and lactation, is also a neurotransmitter in the brain. Scientists have found actions of affection and bonding (hugging, kissing) raise the levels in women and men. Oxytocin also plays a key role in social affiliation, what researchers label as the "tend and friend" response as opposed to the "fight or flight" response.[4]

When a woman asks her partner, "How was your day?" he may have nothing to say unless the workday, the trip, or the visit happens to strike a particular area of interest or significance. When he responds by saying, "Oh, nothing special," he's most likely not intentionally hiding what happened. He just doesn't think much about it, and as a consequence, doesn't remember much.

When a man has little to offer in the way of conversation, a woman will often take it personally, assuming he simply doesn't want to share or is not listening and therefore not responding. In actuality, he may have very little to say and little to offer in return.

With this new insight, a woman can begin to realize that a man is most likely listening and interested in hearing what she has to say. When a woman gives up expecting him to talk more, not only does he appreciate her willingness to talk and stimulate connections in his own mind, but he will also gradually begin to open up.

A gender-intelligent man will turn away from the computer or turn off the television, or put down the paper or smartphone and give her his full attention. If he's under a deadline or feeling stressed, he'll know to say, "I need a few minutes to finish this and I'll be right with you, okay?" He'll let her know that her needs are important and that she's valued, but that he requires a few minutes to sort things out. This simple but sincere gesture on his part will go a long way to reducing her stress and give her the message that he's listening and hasn't checked out completely.

IMPLICIT VERSUS EXPLICIT

It's undeniable that women bring a different perspective and a different value to the workplace. If men understood that another perspective is always the best way to find the best plan of action, and if they would realize that more viewpoints always bring greater success, they would more likely embrace those differences. Success in the workplace requires a blend of broad perspective along with a call to action.

Both men and women use language to bond but do so quite differently. Men will share statistics and facts as a way of connecting, while women will share observations and experiences. You could say that men tend to be more explicit or straightforward with their ideas precisely and clearly expressed, while women have a tendency to be more implicit or indirect, sharing ideas that are implied and suggestively expressed. What's interesting is that men tend to believe their explicitness is the most logical way of thinking and communicating, while women believe their perspective—their implicitness—is the more inclusive approach, for it encourages discussion.

A recent discussion on men's and women's leadership and strategic communication at one of the world's largest financial institutions bears out this difference in gender perspective. The question is: which is the more valued way of thinking and communicating?

The male head of global human resources for the financial institution, in a discussion with the female senior vice president of HR for North America, said, "In our last strategic session, I didn't hear our women leaders from the United States and Canada connecting their arguments and ideas to our top three global strategic priorities."

She responded, "Women leaders *are* connected to the priorities. I didn't sense any disconnection. Yes, the women shifted the discussion with comments that changed the flow of the meeting, but it was the men who thought the women weren't focused on the strategic priorities; the women thought otherwise. They just didn't have a chance to make their case."

In coaching women I often stress that it's a communication style difference for women and a listening style difference for men that we need to bring together in the workplace. Men need to learn the value of incorporating women's connective and consequential way of thinking to enhance problem solving and decision making. Women, though, need to verbally make that link so men can more readily associate the implicit value that women are bringing to that particular topic and to men's linear way of thinking.

Here's an example of what should have been said by the women leaders during the human resources strategy meeting: "One of our top three strategic priorities is innovation, and what I'm about to share with you is directly related to that priority."

THE PERSONAL SIDE OF LIFE: PARTNERS AND PARENTS

In our seminars, women often share that their greatest complaint in their personal relationships is that men don't listen. When a woman doesn't get a chance to talk about her day, she has no avenue by which to release her stress. If her needs are not met, whatever else her partner does for her—whether he's bringing home takeout meals, doing the dishes, or walking the dog after dinner—is experienced through a filter that says she is not getting enough from him.

When a husband and wife do talk, it shouldn't be the way women take turns talking and sharing feelings with another woman. A man simply doesn't think and respond as a woman would. That's precisely why "creating times just to talk" generally doesn't work and tends to be quite stressful for men—because men usually have little to say. He'll start to become restless and irritable, and when he responds to her with these symptoms of resistance or acts distracted, she'll feel even more stressed. To prevent this friction from escalating into a fight, men need to learn the art of listening without interrupting to solve her problems.

But when a man understands he is not expected to share, he is much more willing to listen. If it can make her happy and it doesn't require him to be someone he is not, then he'll become even more willing to listen and actually begin to share more.

It's not only smart, it's an act of loving compassion and kindness for a man to prioritize a woman's need to talk about her feelings before focusing on solving her problems. By recognizing that, his listening will help her feel better and allow her to uncover her own solution to her problem. Just as men need to learn to listen, women need to practice sharing without expecting a man to change in some way. If while sharing, a woman also wants to teach her partner a lesson, improve his behavior, or make him feel bad, it will backfire. He'll feel manipulated by her emotions and eventually be more resistant to listening.

When a woman becomes too involved in how her partner feels or behaves, she tends to become more maternal and goal oriented, taking too much responsibility away from him. This not only weakens him but places more burden on her, and the more likely he's going to tune her out when she talks.

A similar dynamic occurs between mothers and sons, and is exacerbated by how parents interact with each other. Mothers often complain that their sons will not listen to them. This is usually because they are giving too much advice and direction. Mothers often lose the respect of their sons by giving too many orders and then caving in when a son is unwilling to cooperate.

Boys generally need more independence and room to experiment than girls do. They have a greater need to prove what they can do on their own. Too much help from a mother is interpreted as a lack of trust, and eventually the boy stops listening and disconnects.

How a husband treats his wife also makes a big difference in the way a son respects his mother. When the father doesn't respond to the mother's request, it's a clear message that sons don't have to listen either. And, a father should never roll his eyes in front of his son when a mother is making a request. This little gesture may seem harmless on the surface, but it tends to invalidate the mother and teaches boys that it's okay to invalidate women in general in later years.

EIGHT

ARE WOMEN TOO EMOTIONAL?

Women say: "No!"

Men say: "Are you kidding me?"

YES, WOMEN ARE EMOTIONAL, AND THEY TEND TO EXPRESS THEIR experiences—their joys and frustrations, regardless of how large or small—more often than men do. But does that mean that they're *too* emotional? Clearly, women don't think so. And many women believe that men at times simply don't show enough emotion!

Generally speaking, men are just as emotional as women, but tend to conceal their feelings and will only expose that personal side of themselves when they're under high stress, and even then only to people closest to them. Women, on the other hand, tend to express their feelings outright and will openly share their experiences with friends and family alike. Even strangers. Plainly put, women share with others while men tend to seek space and solitude.

STUCK IN TRAFFIC

Let's put this comparison to the test. Rush hour is a stressful irritation experienced all over the world. And the different emotional reactions

GENDER FACTS[1]

- A man will tell up to three people of a negative or positive experience, but only if it's relevant and only if he knows them.
- A woman will tell up to 32 people of a negative or positive experience, even if it's not relevant and whether she knows them or not.

of a man and a woman stuck in traffic—and both very late for an engagement—are no different in Los Angeles, Paris, or Tokyo.

Joe is fuming and, after a minute or two, stops honking his horn. He's still boiling mad at the endless lines of bumper to bumper cars and stoplights. But blaming everyone else on the road isn't working for him, so he quiets down, turns on the radio, and slowly regains his composure. He reasons himself to a state of calmness: "Why does this always happen to me? I won't be caught in this traffic again. Next time, I'll set out earlier."

Anne is in the car right alongside Joe's—and just as late for her meeting. She starts to think about the effect her being late is going to have on certain people at the meeting and the consequences begin to drive up her frustration and stress levels. She calls her friend to share her experience and quell the stress she's feeling: "Julie, you won't believe where I am right now. I'm letting everybody down by being late. I'm so sorry. And that guy in the car next to me honking his horn isn't making matters much better. I wish he'd get a better hold on his emotions!"

When men have strong feelings, they'll externalize the issue and explode if it's a major problem, or become quiet and shut down, especially if there's nothing they can do to immediately resolve the issue. They'll focus on something else to distract their attention away from the problem.

Women don't react as quietly and can't change their focus as easily as men can. They'll tend to personalize the situation—blame themselves—and find others to share their experience with instead of externalizing the problem and blaming out as men do.

So the quick answer to this chapter question—are women too emotional?—is that it's all relative. Men and women simply manage and express their emotions differently. A man at work tends to show very little emotion during the course of his day, whether in team meetings or in one-on-one conversations. This makes it difficult for a woman, or even another man, to get a bead on a man's feelings. A woman, on the other hand, in expressing what she may feel is a moderate and reasonable show of concern for a project or concern for a client, can be misinterpreted by her male colleague as being too emotional. But too emotional compared to whom? Compared to him and how he might react in a similar situation?

At work, one of the biggest problems with the perception that women are too emotional is that a man will tend to avoid a woman expressing her emotions or even attempt to tamp down her feelings by dismissing them out of hand or by rushing in with a quick solution: "Don't worry about it," or "It's not that big a deal."

In doing so, he not only misjudges her reaction, but he misses out on the powerful insights that might be gained from her emotional experience—namely, her access to memories of past events, things he may have forgotten, the value of her experiences whether related or unrelated, and her consequential intuitions whether right or wrong.

WHY WOMEN SHOW EMOTION

There's no denying that both men and women are emotional creatures. Humans have emotions. The difference resides in how each gender expresses their experiences and reactions. Women tend to react with stronger emotions than men do to joy, passion, and problems. In fact, their reactions are often unpredictable to men. He'll assume she's struggling with something major when all she needs is a few minutes to share her joy or alleviate her stress. Men will sometimes express just how lost for words they really are: "She seems really upset. I don't know why, but I'm steering clear." Other times, a man will misread a woman's outburst and assume his role is to swoop in with an immediate solution like, "Don't worry about it," when all she requires is that he listen with interest. Women cope with stress by airing their views and sharing their experiences. This doesn't mean she's complaining or that her issues need to be resolved immediately. Nor does it mean that women are less rational during an emotional moment and can't deal with the problem. Actually, women are far more capable than men of having an emotional outburst and thinking rationally at the same time.

By sharing her experience, a woman is, in a way, listening to herself think. She's able to recall, connect, and release her memories, and, in the process, find a solution and relieve her stress. Not being able to share her feelings with another only prolongs her distress or delays her sense of happiness and well-being.

WHY MEN HIDE THEIR EMOTIONS

Compared to women, men certainly show the world a whole lot less of their emotional side. Men typically feel a need to be self-reliant, and an emotional outburst does not show self-control. This mindset, learned in childhood, is reinforced every day through the social image of the heroic male represented in books and film. Fearless, resourceful, stoic, and usually facing adversity alone, fictional heroes tell us a great deal about what is expected of men, what they expect of themselves, and what is considered ideal male behavior in our society.

More influential than film characters are the roles we see our parents play. Many men have experienced fathers who were emotionally distant, who rarely, if ever, cried or expressed affection. The ways we see our parents and relatives behave in our adolescence are so influential, they become the templates for our own behavior as adults. However, men do have emotions and they express their feelings, but often with less intensity than women.

Here are some examples of situations that we see in business every day, and how men and women will tend to react with different levels and expressions of emotion to the very same experience. Bottom line: women think men don't show enough emotion, and men think women show too much!

Issue/Event	A woman's reaction	A man's reaction
The sales team loses a big client.	"I can't believe we lost it. What did we do wrong . . . what did I do wrong?"	"Companies are watching their budgets. We'll get it next time."
A teammate is let go.	"What will his life be like now? What will happen to his family?"	"Don't worry. He'll land on his feet."
A teammate is promoted.	"I'm so overjoyed for you! We should celebrate!"	"Good for him. I hope I'm next in line."
The company wins a big client.	"Remember the struggle? Everyone should be recognized for their tireless contribution!"	"Hi-fives all around. Now let's win another one!"

The male reaction to stress is to externalize the problem, to try to remain cool and calm, and to focus on a solution. He'll often turn quiet, isolate himself physically, or mentally check out for a period of time, even in the middle of a meeting, and begin his internal process of resolving the issues alone.

When a man is not reacting well to a stressful situation and feels powerless to solve his problem, he'll tend to compensate for showing his emotions by demonstrating his prowess and proving his competence to others. "We're going to get this done, we're going to beat those guys, and we're going to win!" Only if he feels so overwhelmed by the issue will he explode or burst out saying, "This is a problem that we have to find a solution for now!"

Here's the twist on this though. When women are confronted with a problem or issue, great or small, they don't feel the need that men do to compensate for their emotional reaction or to put off addressing the issue to a later time. She's not necessarily feeling inside herself that she's powerless to do anything about it. She's typically thinking, "I still have the power to solve this problem, but I need to connect with my feelings by sharing them with others so I can work this through in my own mind."

"JUST PASS THE TISSUES."

The midyear fiscal planning meeting was probably the worst fiscal experience the company every faced. The recession was having its effect on every aspect of the company's operations. The two women on the budget committee became emotional over the closing of the downtown office and the layoff of over 75 people. Mary, not wanting to show her tears and in a shuddering voice said, "I can't believe we're laying off all those people!"

Mark was quick to react, "Let's take a break and why don't you two gals go to the washroom to compose yourself and we'll continue. Sort yourselves out and come back when you're ready to move on."

Karin responded first, quite upset at Mark's suggestion, "Are you kidding me! That's the last thing we want! I'm not losing it. I'm just expressing how I feel, and I know Mary is doing the same thing. Just pass the tissues and let's go over the numbers again. Maybe we can merge the two divisions at this location and see if we can save money and headcount that way. We're going to lose clients and revenue if we simply let those employees go."

THE SCIENCE SIDE

As we explored in chapter three, women, compared to men, typically have a larger, deeper limbic system—the part of the brain that includes the hippocampus and amygdala, and functions as the hub of emotion and motivation.

The hippocampus is where long-term memory is stored, and although It's typically less active in men, it's larger and far more active in women. This explains why women are more effective at processing and coding emotional experiences into their long-term memory as well as recalling and linking past experiences. The stronger the emotion, the greater the blood flow to the hippocampus and "flooding" of memories. The outcome is a more intense, more vivid, memory-filled emotional reaction.[2]

Even under moderate stress, a woman will generally have eight times the blood flow to the limbic system than men will under the same level of stress. She'll tend to think of everything that can go wrong based on what's happened in the past. She'll feel compelled to talk through her emotions to find a resolution, and as she's talking about it, her stress level will drop.

In comparison, when under moderate stress, a man will generally have minimal blood flow to his limbic system and far fewer neural connections to past memories. Typically, a man would have to be under high stress to register the same level of blood flow in his brain that a woman experiences under moderate stress, and when that happens, it will primarily flow to his amygdala where he'll either deal with the issue or ignore it.

The amygdala in a man's brain is often significantly larger than that of a woman's and has direct neural connections to other response areas in the brain, such as the cerebellum, allowing men to respond rapidly to sensory input, focus on external factors, and take immediate action.

While women tend to internalize, men tend to externalize, not recall past events but concentrate on the situation at hand. Men respond to their environment more quickly than women do because their thoughts are not as filled with emotional connections to past occurrences.

The differences in the limbic systems of women and men have enabled each gender to instinctively protect and defend themselves and others for tens of thousands of years. Women protect through reflection, connection, and cultivation; men defend through quick decision, singular focus, and immediate action unencumbered by emotion.

That's the challenge here, seemingly for men more than for women. Women typically experience a stronger emotional response than men and tend to be more expressive of their reaction. Men often misread the moment and assume her emotions are "getting the best of her" and limiting her ability to think rationally or deal with the pressures of the job.

TRYING TO FIND THE WORDS

On September 11, 2001, women volunteers, talking on the phone with spouses, parents, and children who may have lost their loved ones during the attack on the twin towers in New York, were more able to impart empathy and connect with the family members than the men volunteers were. Many of the men volunteers, although with the best of intentions, found themselves tongue-tied and stammering. They had a difficult time expressing their empathy. They felt compassion but found it hard to find and share the healing words that could comfort the inconsolable in their most desperate moments.

"I COULDN'T CALM HER."

The male volunteers, choking back tears, described their encounters with family members of the victims with specific times and duties, as recounting the facts helped them sort out their intense emotions.

"Our team got the call to assist some of the family members so at 10 A.M. we began taking calls," one man recalls. "Wives, husbands, sons, and daughters were panicking on the phone, telling me what floor their loved one was on and whether he or she was the South or the North tower, and if I knew who the survivors were yet.

"Each was so distraught. I recall one woman who just knew that her husband had died. She was watching the television and watching the replay of the first plane flying right into her husband's side of the tower, at almost the exact floor. I didn't know what to tell her. I couldn't calm her. Then she went completely silent, and I knew I was supposed to say something but all I could say was 'Don't worry, you don't know yet. Don't worry.' I wasn't any good to her," he said as the tears streamed down his face, "but I felt compelled to help."

Men tend to have a difficult time communicating their feelings and because of it are often viewed as inflexible, unfeeling, or uncaring. But it's not necessarily true. Men have feelings, but simply have a harder time connecting with and communicating their feelings than women do. How often do we hear men say, "Of course I care, I just can't find the words"?

"I HAD NO TEARS LEFT, BUT I FOUND THE WORDS."

The female volunteers each seemed to carry the weight of all the family members they spoke with that morning. One woman, whose face was as white as a sheet and shaking, described her encounters that day.

"It was 11:30 A.M. when I received a call from a young girl, an only daughter of a father and mother who both worked in the South tower. It was an hour and a half after the South tower had collapsed and she hadn't heard from her mom or dad yet. We talked for 20 minutes as I helped her first find out whom to contact at the Red Cross for support.

"Then I cried with her for I don't remember how long. I had been crying nonstop since 9 A.M. and I had no tears left, but I found the words for her. I asked her about her other family members, her aunts and uncles. I told her how much they loved her. I told her they would be calling her and to be strong. I told her I would call her back that evening, and she begged me to not let her go but to stay on the phone with her until the Red Cross arrived at her door, and I did."

Women tend to wear many hats, to play many life roles, and are far more adaptive to each situation they encounter. A woman is more able to read the moment and convey her empathy quicker than a man standing in the same room facing the same problem at the same time. So if she's leading others, working on a team, presenting to a client, nurturing a baby, or parenting a teenage son, a woman is more capable of instantaneously immersing herself in the moment and aligning with the feelings of the other person.

Men tend to wear one hat—to live out just one life role—being a man. And men tend to bring that one modality to each situation, whether they are leading, working on a team, talking with male friends, relating with their spouses, or parenting a teenage son or daughter.

It seems that, in every culture, men are prescribed this "one life role" in their adolescence. They're taught by family and society that they are judged by their ability to be strong, to keep their calm, and to not show emotion. This is an unfortunate, limiting disservice to men, who are often incapable of or uncomfortable with sharing their feelings. They frequently feel confused and uncomfortable around a woman sharing hers. It also tends to handicap women in the work-place, who feel they have to hide or hold back their emotions and present themselves as calm and emotionally detached as the men around them in order to show that they too are in control.

Women often say they don't feel comfortable or safe showing their true feelings at work, whether it's happiness, anger, frustration, or fear. They don't ever want to be perceived by the men in the office as being weak or irrational. I can't tell you how many times we've heard women executives say, "Are you kidding me! Never show emotion at work. Never, ever let them see you cry!"

"DON'T EXPECT ME TO SAY 'THANK YOU'!"

As Karin climbed the steps from the train, the morning light made her squint, and as she approached her office building, she knew what she was walking into. She knew that her publishing house would be downsizing across the department, and she would receive word today that she was out of a job. "They'll wait until 4:30 P.M. before telling me," she thought to herself. "They'll get an extra day of work out of me that way."

As she crossed the busy intersection, she played out in her mind how it would happen. "He'll call me into his office and stumble around, trying to find the words to tell me how bad he feels and how much he'll miss me working for him, and how I'll land on my feet real soon." She said out loud, "Don't expect me to say thank you," just so she could hear herself say it. "I'm not going to show any emotion. I'm not! He'll hand me my severance letter and I'll leave."

"I SHOULDN'T HAVE SAID ANYTHING!"

Margaret collected her papers, laptop, and cell phone and headed for the elevators. The Monday morning staff meeting would be the same as every other Monday morning. "I think about these staff meetings every weekend, and they spoil my weekends," Margaret thought to herself. "This is why I don't get any sleep, and Frank thinks I'm upset with him."

She takes her usual seat at the far end of the conference room table and continues her internal dialogue. "The men will want to sit around the department head and fight for his attention. It's not my style. I don't think he likes me anyway. I was the only one to push back on his project last week. It was stupid on my part. I shouldn't have said anything! I won't say anything today.

"The guys on the team always say I'm putting up hurdles to their progress. They think my show of emotion is anger, but it's just concern. I'm not going to show any emotion. But I *am* going to start looking for something else."

It's the lack of gender intelligence in the workplace that often causes a woman to feel that she can't fully express herself, even though she knows what she's feeling is valid. Her natural ability to piece together the pattern of events or outcomes related to an issue or opportunity causes her to be more cautious about the consequences of certain decisions. Still, at times she feels she can't both share her intuition and be considered a team player.

Men are more naturally inclined not to recall past experiences. As action oriented and goal driven as they are, they'll tend to discount or ignore the consequences of their actions and focus solely on achieving their objectives. Their typical attitude is, "Let's just do it and see what happens."

Male decision making tends to be very short term and reactive, and as a result, a man will tend to miss the value of a woman's reflective thinking. He'll tend to misinterpret a woman's reaction as negative and her hesitation as an obstacle to moving forward.

Yes, women are more emotional, but it's a valuable reaction. It's the consequential thinking that's frequently missing in business. The fact that she's raising an issue is not to say she's stopping progress or saying, "No," but is saying, "Consider this first." It doesn't necessarily mean she's complaining or is not as dedicated to the success of a project as the men on her team are, or that the issue she's raising needs to be resolved immediately. She feels compelled to air her views and encourage others on the team to consider all the possible outcomes before making that decision—and maybe make a better decision.

If men can embrace a woman's emotions as an asset, they can be better equipped to anticipate what can go wrong in the future based on what went wrong in the past and possibly discover a better course of action.

Here are a few examples of how a woman may express her ideas with an emotional tone, what she's most likely thinking inside, and how a gender-intelligent man understands and benefits from her reflective thinking.

What she says	What she's thinking	His best reaction
"This will negatively impact too many customers."	"I know there's only a small percentage affected, but it could be indicative of a hidden problem."	"It's worth looking into now instead of having to make costly corrections later."
"This is too risky! We have no proof that it will work."	"I want to get to market as much as you do, but we need more information."	"I don't see the consequences, but you do. There could be liabilities we haven't considered."
"We're making a big mistake."	"It's not my final decision. I'm just having doubts."	"Let me think about this more and then let's talk about it."
"I'm way understaffed! I can't take on the additional work."	"I just want your consideration for all that I'm doing."	"I wasn't aware of the situation. What are our options?"

In each of the examples above, validating a woman's perspective doesn't necessarily mean that a man has to agree with her feelings or intuitions. Her heightened emotional tone may, on the surface, suggest to him that she's feeling negatively, her feelings are final, and her mind is closed, but none of these is necessarily her intention.

A woman's emotional reaction and reflective thoughts can often be the perfect complement to a man's impulse to take immediate action. Men can benefit from taking the time to explore the consequences of their decisions before acting too quickly. And women can gain from the impulse for forward momentum and the ever-present energy offered by the men on their team.

As men and women in the workplace learn to support each other more effectively, emotional tension decreases while cooperation and collaboration increase. The result: better problem solving, enhanced decision making, and greater productivity.

THE PERSONAL SIDE OF LIFE

Women have an enormous capacity to experience and express joy, delight, and fulfillment, even for the smallest things in life. A woman can also feel and convey just as much emotion for the things that bring her stress and anxiety. Whether the emotion is elation or despair, moderate or severe, women feel compelled to share their feelings, especially with their most significant other—their spouse.

Because she wants to talk about an experience—to share what's occurred during her day—it doesn't necessarily mean it's a big deal to her. If it's a joyful emotion and talking about it is her way of reliving that experience with her husband, it can deepen her relationship with him and create a greater sense of intimacy in that shared moment. If it's a worrisome problem, even if only moderately stressful, simply talking about it helps her relieve her stress and, in the process, think things through to her own solution.

Men are not brain wired to recall past experiences—whether good or bad—as easily and vividly as women are. She's looking to share and he may be thinking, "If it's not that big a deal, why is she getting so worked up about it?"

Here are examples of how a woman may share an emotional experience and how her spouse can miss a bonding moment with her. We also show how a thoughtful response can validate her feelings and connect with her in a deeper, more intimate way.

Women have to remember that they make more connections to their emotions and experiences than the men in their life will. And the stronger and more sentimental the emotion, the more memory women will have of that experience. A gender-intelligent woman won't take it personally if her husband doesn't remember the details. Men simply

What she says	How he misses the moment	How he can connect in a deeper way
"Didn't you just love that movie?"	"Yeah, it was alright. Want to get some ice cream?"	"I did. It was a great story! What did you like most about it?"
"I think that was the best salmon dinner I ever prepared."	"You're a good cook. What's for dessert?"	"It came out perfectly! What did you do differently this time?"
"I lost a big client today. Sometimes I don't know if I can make it."	"You worry too much. It's not that big a deal."	"Tell me, what happened?"
"I'm so distressed about having to let my executive assistant go."	"I've fired people in past. Just do it and get past it."	"Is it having to fire her or having to find someone else that distresses you more? Or is it both?"
"Remember when we first had dinner here?"	"No, not really."	"I don't remember. Tell me though!"

don't have as many receptors as women. He's just not designed that way! This doesn't necessarily mean he doesn't care or value her, or that the experience wasn't important to him during the time it happened or even today when she's recalling it. He truly may not remember.

Equally important, a gender-intelligent man will not ignore or dismiss his wife's recollection. Honestly admitting not remembering but also showing genuine interest in reliving the experience can be just as validating for her.

A man tends to forget that a woman's sense and expression of fulfillment is the reason he's drawn to her in the first place; that encouragement lets a man know that he can make a difference in her life.

If a man understands this, he can benefit tremendously in the relationship. When she's talking about her feelings, she's not necessarily looking for solutions. And although his instinct is to solve problems, he really doesn't need to fix anything. At these times, it's not only smart but also respectful for a husband to prioritize his wife's need to talk about her feelings first, before focusing on solutions.

A man listening not only helps a woman relieve her stress, but also helps take the stress out of *his* life. It enables him to take his mind off his own issues, but this only works when he realizes that he doesn't have to solve a problem—just listen and let her express herself. Her emotions heal when they are heard and validated.

NINE

ARE MEN INSENSITIVE?

Women say: "Absolutely!"
Men say: "Some men are, but not me!"

IT SEEMS THAT SINCE THE BEGINNING OF TIME, A MAN HAS RE-
sponded to a woman's claims that he is being insensitive with the
same innocent, perplexed reaction: "No I'm not. . . . How's that? . . .
When?"

Could it be that men don't know what they don't know? That men
can't be sensitive to what they're not sensing to begin with?

Women often read and react to people and environments differently than men do, and they tend to bring more memory and empathy
to virtually every relation and situation. Men are generally not as attentive. That doesn't necessarily mean that they aren't observant. Men
simply tend to take in less, focus only on those things directly related
to an objective, and often do this with far less concern for details.

GENDER FACTS[1]

- 72 percent of women say that men are not as attentive as women
  to people's feelings, situations, and environment.
- 68 percent of men tend to agree.

Add a woman's general ability to remember more, and we have the perfect conditions for the eighth blind spot—that men are insensitive, unmindful of people and situations. The actual blind spot itself is the belief that men are often purposeful in their indifference and forgetfulness. Women often find themselves thinking:

- "How could I have noticed that and you didn't?"
- "You really don't remember?"

A highly successful male business executive put it this way: "I admit that I'm goal driven. Sometimes, it's all I think about when I'm in the office—I focus on the endgame. I really try to read people and situations as best I can, but I know I'm going to miss stuff going on around me. It's not that I'm unconcerned or uncaring; I just don't notice a lot of things."

Men understand, more than ever, that successful leadership requires becoming more perceptive of their environment and mindful of the needs, motivations, and interests of the people around them. Many men today make an effort to be more actively conscious of the people and events around them; nevertheless, being sensitive is not a natural and effortless response for men. Knowing this, a woman can become more understanding when a man appears to be indifferent, self-absorbed, or noncollaborative. She can appreciate that it's more than likely not personal or intentional on his part, but stems from his preoccupation with his own thoughts. She'll even give him a pass for his forgetfulness, though, at times, his absentmindedness may be quite difficult for her to fathom. "How could you forget? We covered it in the meeting this morning!"

Women can also acknowledge that when the heat is on and the stress is high, men will tend to be even less mindful of others and will often fail to notice things, even when they are, literally, in plain sight.

"ALL WE HAVE IS SEVEN MINUTES?"

A workshop we designed for a major toy manufacturer involved an exercise in which five teams of men and women were required to build a model car and a small bridge for the car to travel safely over. The teams had seven minutes to complete the task, which included selling their car and bridge set to the other teams. Each team was videotaped, but within one minute, everyone pretty much forgot that the tape was running!

Given the severe time constraint, most all the men immediately kicked into high gear with focus on chain of command, assignments, and action steps, while most all the women acted less controlling and more suggestive in their ideas. Here's how three of the five teams responded to the challenge:

- "All we have is seven minutes? Give me the instructions," said the senior-most male leader on one team. "Let's see. These are our only materials? Bob, you and Steve start building the car. Mary and Louise, work on the bridge. I'll present. Okay?"
- "I think I know what they're going for," said Julie. "I have an idea and I want to know what you all think."
- "We don't have time for that," said Scott. "Look what Bob and Steve are doing. Ed and Matt, let's go. They're getting ahead of us!"
- "Who here has little kids and knows little toys?" says Monica. "Yes," says Gordon, "That's the way to look at this."

At the end of the exercise, each team reviewed the video of their performance and their interaction with other team members. Each team's overall scores were based on a complex checklist of behaviors and outcomes.

The men were shocked and visibly embarrassed when they saw their actual behavior caught on tape. One man remarked, "I literally pushed her out of the way!" while another noticed that he "didn't even hear her idea. We could have used it to sell the set. I completely ignored her!"

It's amazing how our true nature emerges under pressure. It was a transformational moment for the men and quite insightful for the women. The men were completely unaware of the severity of their take-charge behavior. With only seven minutes, they were in pure action mode and unmindful of everything around them except for winning.

The one team out of the five that did win in the end was the most collaborative in their leadership, teamwork, problem solving, and decision making. They were also the only team in which a man and woman co-presented to the group.

INSENSITIVITY AND THE DRIVE TO WIN

A man's tendency is to be singularly focused and sequential, and to make decisions as quickly as possible. It's a natural, wired-in capacity in men and hugely complementary to a woman's inclination to take in more information and process it through related experiences to formulate a decision. There are pros and cons inherent in both methods, but studies show far greater success when the two mindsets are blended together into one "collective intelligence."[2]

While women care just as much about winning, their need is to achieve greater understanding and cooperation before taking action:

- "Is there an atmosphere of cooperation around me?"
- "Is everybody feeling supported?"
- "Is there tension in the office?"
- "Is everyone participating in the conversation?"
- "Is everyone on board with this decision?"

Independent and comfortable working alone, a man tends not to focus as much on collaboration. Although his intention is to bring his best effort to work each day, his tendencies create a natural blind spot to relational workplace dynamics. For men, it's more a case of self-motivation than group effort. Though men tend to understand and function well with this mindset, it's not a woman's natural inclination. She's more open to building relations and collaborating toward a common goal, and she'll often interpret a male leader's inattentiveness as being more concerned about "winning at all costs" than winning together.

Men, take note, for this is a key aspect in building trust with women: express mutual caring by recognizing and valuing the presence and effort of others. A leader can say he cares, but he'll fall short of demonstrating his best of intentions by being completely absorbed in the goal and unmindful of the seemingly insignificant things going on around him—the little things that can easily add up, or blow up, and ultimately derail his best laid plans.

This is still a challenge for men though. When a man does recognize a situation that requires greater sensitivity, he often doesn't have the skills to navigate in the moment, and he'll resort to showing he cares by doing what he knows best—taking action—when action alone is not always what's needed.

"I THOUGHT I WAS BEING SUPER-SENSITIVE!"

Margot manages a very large creative development department at one of the top ad agencies in New York. Each day is filled with deadlines for copy and graphics, but what she works hardest at is maintaining a sense of balance in the office: "I want my people to meet their deadlines, but not to the point where we lose thoughtfulness and caring for each other. We're most creative when we work together."

Margot is also a mother of twins, and one of her colleagues calls her at home late one morning and catches her with her two sick, young children crying in the background. She told me that she knew James could hear the children crying, but he ignored the situation. "He could have sensed that I had my hands full, but he had to have his question answered. I know he was being his usual task-driven self, which I admire, but he was a little too insensitive.

"I realized that he was not being insensitive but just goal-focused. I had a feeling he was a little uncomfortable calling me at home and discovering the children in the background. The best thing I could do at the time was talk over the kids and give him what he needed so he could move on. He would just have to deal with the noise, and he did. When he sensed I was okay with it, so was he."

I spoke with James afterward and this is how he reasoned it: "I could hear the babies crying but I needed the answer, and I was trying to get it out of Margot as quickly as possible and get off the phone. I needed her direction. I thought I was being super-sensitive and, at the same time, focused on getting the job done. I got the question answered and I was able to deal with the client's issue the way she wanted me to."

There's no changing a man's general competitiveness, and the more aggressive and stressful the profession—whether it's sales, investment trading, law enforcement, event logistics, public relations, entertainment, or criminal law—the more driven he becomes and the less attentive to the needs of others around him.

The insight for men is to show more sensitivity, but, for many men, that's easier said than done. Women have to understand this and not automatically assume that the man is acting deliberately. Women can sabotage their relationship with men by taking offense at something men unknowingly or innocently do, or repeat doing out of forgetfulness.

A man under stress will lessen his anxiety in the best way he knows how—by ignoring the situation or dealing with his problems in solitude. When he reacts this way, whether deliberately or involuntarily, he's often not being purposefully callous or uncaring. And when women react with that belief and take offense, it can be just as offending to him. "Of course I care, what gives you the impression I don't?"

INSENSITIVITY IN DISCUSSION

Women say that men are most insensitive when it comes to communication—when men take a hard and fast position, state their opinion for all to hear, and in the process discourage any further discussion. Here are some frequently used phrases that signal a shutdown of discussion:

- "I know my plan will work."
- "We don't have time to discuss it."
- "We need to move now if we're going to make the deadline!"

Although a woman may have her own position already thought through, her inclination is not to give her opinion as much as it is to encourage ideas from others. Her tendency is to have everyone weigh in before she'll share her thoughts. She'll feel more comfortable with a decision knowing first that all ideas have been explored.

Men tend to see this differently. They believe they are performing at their peak by offering their best ideas without hesitation. They also believe that if others have something to say, they'll speak up without being prodded. A man feels he is being sensitive by not putting another person on the spot, so he avoids asking directly for other opinions.

Many male business leaders have learned to sharpen their perception, to come out of their comfort zones, and to recognize the value of not being so immediately reactive. They'll intentionally seek out the input of their female colleagues to ensure there are no underdeveloped ideas or hastily drawn decisions.

What she says	How he shows insensitivity	His better reaction
"I think we should review all the available data before we move forward."	"This is not a complicated decision. We already know everything we need to know."	"Perhaps we should carve out more time on the agenda for analysis."
"I feel like we're still missing something."	"All the facts have been presented. We've already made plans."	"It may not be too late. What are you thinking?"
"I don't think everyone on the team has bought into this."	"They had a chance at the last meeting. They should have said something then."	"Let's make sure we have everyone's buy-in, but to stay on schedule, let's give them until end of week. Does that work for you?"
"We took that approach in the last sales drive and it didn't work."	"I don't remember that happening. It doesn't matter, the situation was different."	"I didn't think of that. What was the situation then? Why do you think it didn't work?"

In each of the examples above, the clear challenge for men is not to become so easily frustrated with too many details, to remain open-minded, and not to state their conclusions or solutions so quickly. A gender-intelligent man will relax the pace a bit. He'll be less competitive and less self-absorbed in his thinking. He'll realize that where he may be weakest is exactly where a woman may be strongest—in her abilities to recall past experiences, to weigh consequences with sound judgment, and to offer alternative ideas.

A gender-intelligent woman will understand that men don't naturally share their thought processes and are more comfortable thinking through issues alone. She'll understand that a man's tendency for action is a perfect complement to her inclination to question. The

challenge is for both genders to realize that the best decisions lie somewhere in the intersection of their natural thought processes.

INSENSITIVITY IN E-MAILS AND TEXT MESSAGES

It should come as no surprise that, just as women tend to share more
information, build relations, and ask more questions than men do
when communicating face to face, women are more inclined to behave
the same way in their e-mails and texts messages. It should also come
as no surprise that men will often bring their "let's get to a decision"
style of communication to their written messages as well.

There's no tone of voice in an e-mail or a text message, just words,
lying there flat on the page, void of context and perspective. In this
format, a man's tendency for brevity can come across as critical and
uncompromising to a woman, while he'll interpret his own short comments as "brief and to the point."

On the next page are examples of written exchanges between a
male leader and a female department head over the need to complete a
client proposal before a Friday afternoon deadline. This shows how his
written messages can be interpreted as indifferent and uncaring, and
how a more thought-out communication with a more collaborative
tone can lead to greater understanding and better results.

INSENSITIVE HUMOR

As we explored in chapter four, joking is a way men commonly test
friendships with other men, allowing them to be critical of each other
but in a light-hearted, off-the-cuff way. It's part of the male bonding ritual as well as a man's way of letting off steam or diffusing a
tense situation. A man will occasionally toss out a sarcastic remark or
playful insult and then say, "Just kidding!" or "Just joking!" The man
on the receiving end of the disparaging remark usually won't take it

What he sends	How she reads the message	His better communication
"The proposal is due Friday at 5 P.M. Get it to me Thursday afternoon."	"He must be upset with me about something. How do I ask for his input to be certain I'm on track?"	"I'd like you to take the lead on this proposal. Please send me a draft by Thursday afternoon. I'll build on it and get it back to you to finalize Friday morning."
"Have your department complete this ASAP!"	"This doesn't have to go out until Friday afternoon and my staff is buried in work. Am I supposed to drop everything?"	"Please review the attached. We have a few days to complete this proposal. Let's discuss at your earliest convenience."
"This is not what I was looking for."	"I thought we were going to collaborate on this and mine was a first draft."	"This is coming together! Please review my attached edits and comments and let me know what you think."

personally. If he does, his reaction immediately sets the limitation to their friendship.

There are all kinds of zingers or little digs that men will good-naturedly level at each other, such as:

- "Did you really mean to wear that? You must dress in the dark!"
- "Don't forget your GPS. You'll probably get lost again!"
- "Why would I want to have lunch with you?"
- "You're an idiot! Why would you even vote for that person?"

Imagine a man directing any one of these taunts to a woman instead of another man! This sort of humor tends to be lost on women who relate to and bond with other women in a completely different way. A woman doesn't easily comprehend men's humor. It commonly comes across as a complete waste of time for her and lands as just another example of a man's insensitive nature.

"WHAT A RUDE GUY!"

Years ago, during a midmorning break at a workshop in Germany, a senior executive attending the session began sharing with me how much he enjoyed the morning focus group. Halfway into our conversation, he started tossing an apple back and forth from one hand to the other while his eyes occasionally scanned the room. I thought to myself, "What a rude man! Is he bored with this conversation? Am I boring him? Or is he just trying to act cool and nonchalant?" His physical activity was actually distracting me. I found myself focusing on the apple instead of what he was saying.

As I discovered later, his physical actions may have been distracting to me but not to him! He was actually making every attempt to be in the moment with me.

When a man is feeling anxious or stressed out, his adrenaline increases, and the smallest of physical activity can help convert his adrenaline into dopamine. Dopamine is a simple chemical—a neurotransmitter—produced in several areas of the brain and is responsible for modulating physical movement as well as regulating aggression, motivational drive, and the restraint or control of an impulse. Physical movement actually calms the male brain so he can focus on his work, listen more intently, or collect and share his thoughts.[3]

Men often tune out in the workplace or in meetings when there is a lot of discussion. So to stay alert, a man will tap his pen or his foot, or gaze around the room, and in the process regain his calm and focus. So the man flinging the apple from hand to hand wasn't being inattentive or showing boredom. Quite the contrary: he was trying to maintain his focus on our conversation!

THE SCIENCE SIDE

Research shows that men are often not as adept at reading facial expressions and emotional nuances as women are. This ability also enables women commonly to sense and emulate what the other person is experiencing through a process called mirroring. Women have special neurons that enable them to be human emotion detectors. Brain scans show that women can more effectively mirror the feelings of another person than men typically can.[4]

From birth, males and females tend to show different environmental scanning abilities: females spend more time scanning the faces around them while males focus on their environment. When a woman carefully scans a face, she often picks up micro-expressions apparent in the facial muscles, mouth, and rate and depth of breathing. Micro-expressions reveal the universal human emotions of anger, fear, sadness, disgust, contempt, surprise, and enjoyment, which are present for a split second but are important in order to communicate and understand others with greater sensitivity.

Brain scan studies indicate that the female brain generally has larger areas—specifically the insular cortex, the anterior cingulated cortex, and the corpus callosum—that enable them to "read" interpersonal experiences, be more empathetic toward others, and track gut feelings.[5]

The insular cortex, often called the insula, is a portion of the cerebral cortex that is believed to be involved in consciousness. It plays a role in the diverse functions usually linked to emotion or the regulation of the body's homeostasis. These functions include perception, motor control, self-awareness, cognitive functioning, and interpersonal experience. The insula is often approximately twice as large in women than in men, giving women a broader ability to be more sensitive to mood and ambiance.

The anterior cingulate cortex is the frontal part of the cingulate cortex and resembles a collar around the corpus callosum. The ACC is typically larger in women than in men and plays a role in a wide variety of autonomic functions, such as regulating blood pressure and heart rate, as well as rational cognitive functions, such as anticipation, decision making, empathy, and emotion. As a result, women tend to weigh options, reflect (ruminate), and feel and express concern often at greater depths than men.

In chapter four, we described the corpus callosum as being 25 percent larger in a woman's brain than in a man's. Having more neural connections between both hemispheres of the brain enables women to engage in right-brain and left-brain activities simultaneously, while men tend to use either side of their brain sequentially. A larger corpus callosum also enables women to understand the unspoken components of a conversation, i.e., read body language, tone of voice, and facial expressions, more effectively than men are able to. As a result, women tend to take in a broader, more inclusive perspective of situations and view the elements of a problem or task as interconnected.

The size and interrelationship of these brain parts in women—the insular cortex, the anterior cingulated cortex, and the corpus callosum—may tend to heighten their perception and intuition, making women far more sensitive than men to the feelings and ambiance of people and events around them.

There's another dynamic occurring here. When women communicate, they tend to look directly at each other throughout their conversation. The more intent women are, the more they focus on each other's eyes. A man, on the other hand, will tend to look away to stimulate his thinking process as he asks himself, "What's the solution to this?" His inclination is not to maintain eye contact while he's searching for an answer or lending greater concentration to the discussion. Instead, he'll look up or over or down, or even cock his head to the side.

Another man will be comfortable with this behavior and think, "He must be focusing intently about what I'm talking about," while a woman's personal reaction will be, "Hello in there! He's so easily distracted. He probably doesn't even care about what I'm saying."

If a woman understands a man's intention, she's going to take it less personally when he's juggling an apple or tapping a pen on a table, or shifting uncomfortably around in his seat, or looking around while she's talking.

On the other hand, a gender-intelligent man has to be more conscious of the fact that physical movements that help him remain focused could be sending her just the opposite message—that she's taking too long to explain something or that he's not that interested in what she's talking about.

WOMEN'S INSENSITIVITY TO MEN

Although this chapter centers on how women at times consider men insensitive, there are times in which a man would consider a woman's reaction as an inaccurate and unfair read of his behavior. Although men won't commonly show their vulnerable side and even mention this, they do open up in our workshops and seminars and mention the ways in which they believe women show insensitivity:

- Correcting a man in the presence of others is highly embarrassing to a man. So embarrassing that he typically doesn't know how to respond in that situation. He'll often just freeze in place and find himself at a total loss for words. The gender-intelligent thing for a woman to do is to raise the issue at another time and in private, when she can let him know how she experienced his behavior and he can have an opportunity to reflect and respond.
- Offering a man unsolicited advice is to presume that he doesn't know what to do or that he can't do it on his own. The issue of competence is very important to a man. Men tend to handle their problems on their own; however, if he truly does need help, and assuming he trusts her to be a resource for him rather than a critic who wants to correct or change him, he'll ask her for her feedback and advice.
- Generalizing that "all men behave that way" tends to make a man feel blamed for something he didn't do or wouldn't think of doing. Though there are men who can act exclusionary or dismissive to a woman, there are many who make an effort to

act inclusively and with understanding. Men often want to be seen as the solution and not to be painted with such a broad brush.

- Suggesting that men don't notice as much as a woman notices makes men feel less capable. The reality is that men and women notice different things, and women tend to notice far more than men do. It's not that men aren't attentive and therefore don't care; they just are not as tuned in as women are.

In virtually every instance, a man's belief that a woman is being insensitive stems from her taking offense for something he did, when offense was never intended on his part in the first place.

EQUAL LEARNING ON BOTH SIDES

The bottom line of this chapter, as it is with all eight gender blind spots, is that there is equal opportunity for learning by both genders. What choice do we have but to find our paths to success in the workplace together?

It's not enough for a man to simply say, "I'm just being myself," and not make an effort to connect more deeply with his coworkers and to read situations around him with heightened awareness. Just because a man isn't hardwired to be as sensitive as a woman doesn't mean he can't become more observant of his own behavior and demonstrate greater care and consideration for others. Given that half of today's workforce is made up of women and companies have become blends of so many different cultures, successful leadership requires a greater level of active consciousness and personal engagement.

Gender intelligence will help a woman understand that what she may perceive as insensitivity or lack of care on the part of a man is most likely not intentional. This understanding can help her to become more direct in her interactions and to frame her conversations in ways that will ensure her male coworkers are more aware of her meaning, needs, and expectations. He'll show greater appreciation for her acceptance of him and for not taking offense at his occasional inattentiveness. He'll return her show of understanding with his show of trust in her and express greater interest in cooperating and collaborating with her.

Here are examples of how men can become more receptive to the spoken and unspoken reactions of their women colleagues. This chart isn't intended to cover the waterfront of emotions and situations, but rather to give examples of the ways a man can begin to close the gap in his attentiveness and, as a result, enrich his professional and personal life.

Her communication	His gender intelligence	His best reaction
She's not saying anything during a meeting.	A woman's mind is seldom if ever inactive! She's most likely waiting to be included in the conversation.	"I'm interested to know what your thoughts are on this."
"I'm fine."	Her giving a short answer often means things may not be fine.	"I may be misinterpreting, but are you really fine?"
"You didn't do what I asked."	He doesn't immediately become defensive but seeks greater understanding.	"I may have missed something. What would you like me to do?"
"What's everyone else thinking?"	He knows that she's unlikely to be uncertain but is seeking collaboration, so he doesn't automatically take charge.	"Let's open this up to discussion."

When a man asks, "How are you?" and she responds with a quick and short, "I'm fine," she's going to assume that he can read between the lines and draw her out more. It's much harder for a man to read facial expressions and voice inflections, so he'll usually take her words literally and respond with something like, "Great, glad to hear it."

What a misread on both their parts! She'll most likely conclude, "He doesn't really care," while he stands there, oblivious to her true meaning, and assumes that everything is okay with her. It's not that he doesn't care. It's more likely that the whole thing went right over his head!

If a woman were to ask another woman, "How are you?" and she responds with the short answer, "I'm fine," the inquiring woman is going to sense that things are perhaps not okay and will most likely take a step closer, lend her full attention, and probe a little deeper with a sincere, "You don't sound okay. What's going on?"

THE PERSONAL SIDE OF LIFE

Whether they are children, adolescents, or young adults, sons and daughters share stressful experiences with their parents in completely different ways. If a daughter is confronted with a pressing issue, she'll be more inclined to want to sit and talk through her problem in great detail. She'll begin talking to find her focus and, at times, will start her conversation from what will appear to be a totally unrelated place, as in this example:

"When I was driving home Saturday night, and I didn't mean to keep the car out that late, and it won't happen again Dad, but it wasn't my fault really, because I had to take Mona and Charlie home first since Mona's car wouldn't start. Anyway, I was driving home and I started worrying about finding a job during the school year . . ." And she'll eventually get to the point she's trying to make.

This process allows her to focus in on her priorities and gain clarity on the most important issue or issues that she needs to resolve in her own mind. A composed mother will tend to understand what "talking to focus" is all about, and she will sit there patiently and let her daughter process her thoughts without interruption.

Fathers, on the other hand, often alienate their daughters by offering snap solutions and not asking enough questions. Men commonly don't understand that their daughters are not always looking for advice or help. They mistakenly assume that their job is to swoop in and fix it, when much of the time, a young girl, teenager, or woman will just want to be heard. The truth is, a father cares about his daughter's well-being, which is why he works so hard for her happiness and will always feel compelled to rush in and solve her problems. What she wants from her dad, though, is his patience and sensitivity for the little things that mean so much to her.

The most sensitive, caring thing a dad can do is to encourage his daughter to share her experiences with him and simply listen while offering the occasional, "Uh huh," "I see," or "Okay." A sensitive father will turn off the television, put down the smartphone, look away from the computer screen, quit tinkering with the light fixture, and give his daughter the few minutes of his full attention—which is all she's asking for!

The most insensitive thing a dad can do is continue doing whatever he's doing and stop her short with, "Can you just get to the point?" or "That's not important," or "Don't worry about it so much."

Sons, on the other hand, don't feel the same compulsion to share their feelings. Under moderate stress, a boy, teenager, or young man will want to work through the issue on his own and find his own solution. But if the son is experiencing higher stress, a parent will stand a better chance of getting him to open up if the two of them engage in some kind of activity to stimulate conversation and sharing, such as going for a walk, or throwing a ball, or doing some task together. As daughters will often talk to find their focus, sons will find their focus first before sharing—and physical activity actually helps boys concentrate and center their thoughts.

Fathers and mothers today have less time than ever to devote to parenting. So often a man is driven to be the provider for his family, thinking that his hard work is all that's expected of him. Yet, with his nose to the grindstone, he's missing the moments that truly matter to his children and unknowingly depriving them of what they crave the most—his time and attention.

GROWING IN OUR
GENDER INTELLIGENCE

TEN

BUILDING TRUST WITH WOMEN, INCREASING CREDIBILITY WITH MEN

THROUGHOUT OUR BOOK, WE SHARED HOW MEN'S AND WOMen's assumptions and opinions of each other get in the way of their working and succeeding together. We found that recognizing and dispelling our blind spots and understanding and valuing our gender differences are the important firsts in creating professional and personal relationships that are built on a foundation of trust.

Trust must be present before we willingly open ourselves up to greater understanding and acceptance. It's the most effective way of relating to others, working with others, and getting results. We each want to be trusted, we respond to trust, and we thrive on it!

Over the years, we have discovered in our workshops that women and men have differing notions about the meaning of trust and what it takes for the other gender to earn their trust.

Women say: "The way men build trust with me is by demonstrating their caring—by showing genuine interest in me and valuing my ideas. By making an effort to understand what motivates me and by working with me."

Men say: "The way women build trust with me is through their credibility and capability—by recognizing and appreciating my true intentions and working with me to find solutions that get results."

Although there is an underlying difference in that women generally seek caring while men seek capability, there are two needs that are commonly shared by both genders: men and women want to be understood and valued for their authentic selves, and both want to create and maintain bonds at work that will enable them to perform and succeed together.

Whether at work or in personal life, a woman will consider a man worthy of her trust when he shows care and concern for the things that matter most to her:

- "I want to trust that you will include me and value my opinions."
- " . . . that you are genuinely listening."
- " . . . that you'll understand my emotions."
- " . . . that you'll give me honest feedback."

Men are often not aware of how important it is to build and maintain that level of trust with women. A man without gender intelligence may hear her say these things but miss her point completely. There's the blind spot! Men usually don't know what women are looking for in a trusting relationship and often fail to recognize how vitally important it is to them. To complicate matters, many women don't often understand how unaware men truly are, which is why women continue to expect some sort of breakthrough to occur—and why men often misread the situation completely and continue to play by their own rules.

INSIDE-OUT CONGRUENCE

Once a man build trusts with a woman, any misunderstandings, mistakes, or differences that are certain to arise will appear as mere blips on the screen and will not rock that foundation of trust. This is not to suggest that men have carte blanche in their behavior! For women, trust is based on integrity, and the way to show integrity is through congruent, consistent behavior—whether in private or in public.

This can be very challenging for a man who can easily find himself caught up in the male code of behavior at work and consequently shows a lack of congruency by:

- Sexually objectifying women with jokes or comments.
- Excluding women from meetings or discussions.
- Dismissing a woman's questions or ideas.

He may not actually participate in the behavior himself, but remember, a man's first inclination is not to put another man on the spot. Not wanting to rock the boat by challenging the male code, he may not say anything to the other man showing offensive behavior, or excluding her, or dismissing her ideas. And waiting until later to express his "indignation" doesn't quite cut it. He will know he has eroded that foundation of trust with her when she says, "I can't believe he said that in front of you. Why didn't you say something?"

Although many men today are conscientious enough not to objectify women, it takes a great deal of courage for a man to correct another man's behavior in public, especially in mixed company. Nevertheless, gender-intelligent men find ways to take the lead and teach other men by example—through their own congruent behavior or by stepping up and calling them on it.

GENDER FACTS[1]

- 95 percent of men and women consider trust to be the foundation of a working relationship.
- 92 percent of women say men earn their trust through caring and concern.
- 89 percent of men say women earn their trust by showing credibility and competence.

"I THOUGHT I KNEW THIS GUY!"

Anne and Phyllis left the restaurant in total disbelief. Lunch with Peter was nothing like it used to be back in graduate school. It was a little less than a year since all three received their degrees and ventured out to make their way in the working world. They were both happy for Peter, who had landed a great position with that prestigious company, but by the time the waiter brought the appetizer, the two women realized they were having lunch with a total stranger.

Anne was first to break the silence, "I used to think Peter was the most sensitive and caring man I ever knew. He always showed interest in what I was saying. He seems so self-absorbed now. I really thought I knew this guy!"

Phyllis agreed. "He talked about himself throughout lunch! Sure, he asked us what we were up to, but then, did you notice? He kept checking for messages the whole time you talked about your new job."

"And he acted surprised that you were heading up that project, like it was over your head or something," Anne added. "I feel a real loss here. We went through some real tough times together. We had each other's backs back then."

For many men, college life and work life are worlds apart. There's a shift that seems to take place in men. They tend to be much more flexible and open-minded when they're in that learning environment, but once they migrate into the work world, another dynamic takes over and they feel compelled to compete. They're quick to adapt to the male hierarchy and the male code of behavior at work. Women tend not to change that way or that drastically. For them, the camaraderie and collaboration continues at work, but unfortunately more often with women than with men.

Nevertheless, there are men who tend to show the same, consistent behavior from their college years throughout their working lives. They make great strides in establishing and maintaining a trusting relationship with the women they work with. Women recognize this, and in our workshops, consistently cite the top ways men earn their trust:

- "By valuing my contribution."
- "By including me in formal and informal settings."
- "By acknowledging my questions."
- "By genuinely listening."

VALUING CONTRIBUTIONS

While men thrive on being recognized for their results, women feel most appreciated and validated when they're acknowledged for the challenges they face in the attainment of those results. For many women, recounting the journey and being valued for their participation is as significant and personally fulfilling as arriving at the destination.

This is often very difficult for men to understand because men tend to be so results driven. What men don't usually understand is that what a woman *does* to achieve an objective needs to be acknowledged and valued as much as men need to be acknowledged and valued for actually achieving the objective. This is not to say that women aren't goal driven or that men don't value relationships. Men and women simply have different orientations toward achievement.

Gender-intelligent men recognize that a woman's sense of appreciation can differ from that of their male colleagues, and they actively build trust with their women coworkers by showing that they understand and value that difference in both great and small ways.

Consider these general similarities and differences in how women and men feel appreciated and validated.

What women appreciate	*What men appreciate*
Choosing her as part of a team to accomplish a task.	Asking him to work on a project independently.
Offering her unsolicited support to show care and interest.	Not offering him unsolicited support to show confidence in his capabilities.
Asking her questions throughout the process to maintain an atmosphere of collaboration.	Letting him know that you're available if questions arise.
Drawing her out by encouraging her participation during meetings.	Not drawing him out but knowing that if he has something to say, he'll share when he's ready.
Recognizing her challenges and contribution during the process.	Rewarding his results.

INCLUSIVENESS

A woman's sense of not being included is not about an occasional occurrence or a specific instance, but rather a habitual pattern of male behavior at work. Men tend not to see it but it's there—this drip, drip, drip of men's repetitive behavior that tends to ignore or dismiss a woman's participation during meetings, prevents her from participating in informal networks, and impedes her chances of benefiting from valuable mentoring opportunities. A gender-intelligent man who breaks through this often-unintentional but ever-present barrier of exclusion and shows that he "has her back" will forever have her trust and support.

Here's one example that always comes up during our workshops—something that men do that may seem small but eats away at a woman's sense of partnership and trust.

A group of men are sitting in the conference room before the meeting starts. They're talking about some male-oriented subject and laughing when a woman walks in and the room suddenly goes quiet. The men are searching for something else to say to bridge the silence but come up short. That moment of silence is so frustrating to her. She's been there many times before. She acts indifferent, but there's no real sense of trust and camaraderie. What is she left to believe? That she's interrupting a bonding session? That the conversation is about her? That she's outside the circle?

A gender-intelligent man will be the first to bridge the conversation and make her feel included. She'll trust him more than the others because he's attentive. He recognizes the situation and acts accordingly. If the conversation is objectifying, he won't be joining in. That kind of male behavior is so last-century to him. His nonparticipation sends messages to the other men that it's a callousness that's juvenile and beneath him.

There are a number of ways gender-intelligent men include women and build a foundation of trust. It takes active consciousness on the part of men and a concerted effort to look around their own blind spots.

Encourage her participation.
A male team leader will tend to ignore a man who has not spoken during a meeting. He'll assume the man quietly sitting there doesn't have anything of value to offer at that moment, and he won't put him on the spot. He'll know that women tend to view team participation

differently, and that they most likely expect to be invited to partici-pate. He'll immediately make this distinction and ask the women to share their ideas.

Acknowledge her ideas and questions during meetings.
Men typically collaborate to compete and tend to approach teamwork as a team sport. Men often build on each other's ideas, best each other, and don't feel the need to give credit during the exchange. A gen-der-intelligent man will recognize that women are not that into one-upmanship and will often credit them during the exchange of ideas.

Invite her to informal events.
Many informal networks and events have been traditionally de-signed around men's interests, and though women don't necessar-ily want to prevent men from engaging in male-related activities, they do want to feel a part of the team. A gender-intelligent man will genuinely invite a woman and let *her* accept or decline the in-vitation, instead of assuming no interest on her part. And given that half the workforce today is comprised of women, gender in-telligence suggests designing some social events that center around men's and women's interests.

ACKNOWLEDGE QUESTIONS

A gender-intelligent man generally doesn't view a woman's questioning as impulses that need to be tolerated, minimized, or even avoided by strategically navigating around sensitive issues. He finds it a valuable instinct, complementary to his way of thinking.

The chart on the next page shows how a gender-intelligent man is typically more attentive to the significance of her questions and responds in a way that encourages inquiry but is balanced with a pro-clivity to action.

What she asks	What she may really be saying	How he acknowledges her questions
"Shouldn't we think more about the outcome before we make the decision?"	"I'm concerned that we may be making a mistake."	"You're having reservations about this. What do you think might be some of the consequences?"
"May I ask a question?"	"I may have a better idea."	"Of course. I want to know what you're thinking is on this."
"Do you think the conference is worth my attending?"	"I'm not sure if I want to attend or not."	"What are you hoping to get out of it?"
"Are you alright in preparing this presentation?"	"I'm here if you need me."	"Once I have the first draft, I'd like to run it past you for your ideas."

Women often have a different line of sight into situations and events than men do because of their capacity for relational and consequential thinking. It is an instinctive response that women have to the world around them and one of their best contributions—one that men often and mistakenly disregard. A gender-intelligent man regards her reservations about a pending decision as an intuitive feeling that may be well worth investigating before a decision is made.

GENUINELY LISTEN

When a man shows himself to be distracted, either by not looking directly at a woman when she's talking with him, fidgeting with his watch, looking around the room, or checking his phone for e-mail messages, a woman tends to take it personally. She will tend to conclude, "He's not interested in what I'm saying," or "I'm not that important to him."

Even though he may be listening or trying his best to listen, the gender-intelligent man will realize that his physical behavior may suggest that his thoughts are elsewhere. He recognizes his behavior is not giving the right signals, and he'll turn away from the computer, or turn off the television, or put down the paper or cell phone, and give her his full attention.

If he's under a deadline or feeling stressed, he'll know to say, "I need a few minutes to finish this and I'll be right with you." He will let her know that her needs are important and that she's valued, but that he requires a few minutes to sort things out. This simple but sincere gesture on his part will go a long way to reducing her stress. It sends the message that he cares, and that when he is engaged, she can trust that he'll be listening with his full attention.

Women tend to have a much greater tolerance for emotional distress than men do. With this higher threshold, they can patiently listen to another's issues without feeling an urgency to parachute in with a solution. A man hears a problem and his tendency is to do something about it immediately.

When he reacts with, "I understand" or "Don't worry about it," what she hears is either, "I heard enough and here's my solution," or "I don't want to listen anymore—let's change the subject."

An attentive man realizes that she most likely wants him to hear all of what she has to say before offering his point of view. He also realizes that she may not want his perspective but just someone to listen as she thinks the issue through. Instead of saying, "I understand" right away, he assures her that he's listening by occasionally nodding and making acknowledging sounds such as, "Oh," "Yes," or "Hmmm."

When a man listens without judgment but with empathy and relatedness to a woman expressing her thoughts, she feels heard and understood. She trusts him to be her sounding board and confidant— someone she can come back to, time and again.

UNDERSTAND EMOTIONS

We often talk about emotions in the workplace as if they don't belong there or that the workplace should be an environment of only reason and logic, when, in reality, virtually everything we do at work is driven by emotions.

A gender-intelligent man often understands the value of emotion in the workplace. He understands that many of the key drivers of employee engagement—such as finding meaning and purpose in one's work, or pride in the company's products or services—are often sustained at an emotional level. He doesn't shy away from displays of emotion. He realizes that attempts to hold back a woman's experiences and reactions may be restraining her passion for her work or impeding her desire to offer her best.

He frequently gives her the feedback she wants instead of holding back. If she becomes emotional, even to the point of tears, he validates her feelings and shows his understanding: "I can see that this is really important to you," or "Is there any way that I can have a role in helping with this?"

He doesn't tamp down or dismiss her experiences or reactions out of hand, or rush in with a quick solution such as, "Don't worry about it" or, "It's not that big a deal." He realizes that she's not asking him to solve her issue—that she most likely has the power and the wherewithal to solve it herself, and that she is connecting with her feelings by sharing them.

He commonly realizes that women have the capacity to show emotion and logic simultaneously—something that men have a greater difficulty doing. He considers her emotional reaction during a meeting as an expression of passion rather than one of anger or uncertainty. He doesn't end the meeting or avoid her for the balance of it, but he continues to acknowledge that her expression may be rich in insights, related experiences, and necessary judgments.

In previous chapters, we focused primarily on the differences in the brain architecture of men and women and how our physiological differences contribute to the dissimilar ways men and women think and behave. Another differentiating element of male and female biology that plays a key role by activating and connecting the various parts of our brain are neurotransmitters that carry messages, trigger responses, and create emotional states that either increase or reduce stress.

As we go about our lives, these neurochemicals are constantly shifting, prompted by what's happening in our brains. The brain takes in sensory information and processes it. It sends a burst of molecules, some in the form of hormones through the bloodstream, that mobilize the body to react. Oxytocin is one such neurochemical that enters the bloodstream in the form of a hormone. "For decades, scientists thought its role was limited to childbirth and breastfeeding. They had no idea of its effects on emotions."[2]

Today, oxytocin is often referred to as the social attachment hormone. While this powerful hormone is found in both men and women, it generally plays a more essential role in a woman's life. In addition to stimulating maternal behavior in women, oxytocin has a calming effect on women's emotions.

Research has shown that levels of oxytocin in women increase when they connect with someone through trust, friendship, caring, and nurturing.[3]

There is a direct correlation between the support a woman feels and the maintenance of a high level of oxytocin. How a woman interprets her partner's actions will determine her level of oxytocin.

In females and males, oxytocin typically brings about personal relaxation as well as bonding with each other. To maintain this sense of fulfillment, the brain needs repeated activation stimulated by closeness, touch, and conversation. Males actually need to have physical contact two to three times more frequently than females do to maintain the same level of oxytocin. Couples may not realize how much they depend on each other's physical presence until they are separated for extended periods. When partners are apart, the lack of frequent touch for men and touch, conversation, and sharing of experiences for women depletes the brain's oxytocin levels. Partners are often drawn to each other to replenish their nurturing hormone and experience again pleasure, comfort, and contentment.[4]

If a woman finds she can share her thoughts with a man who makes an effort to understand the nature of her feelings, she'll trust him. And she will remember him as someone she can confide in, knowing he'll listen with interest and empathy.

INCREASING CREDIBILITY WITH MEN

Women tend to place their trust in a man who shows that he cares, values her contribution, includes her, and listens with genuine interest and empathy. And just as men have their blind spots in understanding how important it is to build and maintain trust with a woman, women are often blind to what encourages a man to place his trust in her. Moreover, what makes it difficult for women to know what it takes to earn a man's trust is that he doesn't often communicate his feelings, needs, and expectations.

What we've learned through our workshops is that, for a man, trust is all about credibility—aligning with his goals, believing in him, and helping him succeed. In our workshops, men often cite these characteristics that prompt them to trust a woman:

- "Doesn't try to correct me or change me."
- "Helps me achieve my goals."
- "Realizes that I'm interested and listening."
- "Doesn't automatically assume that I'm insensitive or don't care."

It's a challenge for a woman to establish her career and ascend in a male-designed and male-dominated working world with her authenticity intact, but it's not impossible. The one thing that women should realize about men is that it's the results that matter most to them—more than the challenges faced or the relationships made along the way.

The fact that the journey and the relationships are important to her doesn't mean that there's a chasm here that can never be bridged. A woman can be just as ambitious and goal-oriented as the men around her, which is why a woman aligning with a man's goals can be authentic for her yet supportive of him.

A man will place trust in a woman who understands, aligns with, and acts upon those things that matter most to him—achieving the results and winning. If she emphasizes alignment with his objectives, he'll forever seek her out as a trusted colleague. If that connection isn't made, his inclination will be to work independently or align with someone else who can help him succeed.

"YOU DON'T GET TO TELL ME WHAT TO DO!"

There are many great executive coaches, but the best ones are those who advise their clients to be gender-intelligent when building a foundation of trust among subordinates, peers, and superiors. Michele didn't receive that level of coaching and ended up learning some new things about what it takes to earn the trust of her male superiors. Her coach told Michele to approach her interview for the promotion as a man would: "Study the situation, collect the facts, and present your solutions with confidence."

Michelle did just that. In fact, she did what many women tend to do—she overprepared. She had all the facts and figures on her industry, her company's position, its challenges, and the opportunities. For the entire hour, she inundated her future boss and his boss with issues and solutions. But throughout that hour, all the two men heard was, "Here's what you're doing wrong and what you need to fix."

Michelle confided afterward, "I started to feel it going south halfway through the interview, but I didn't know why. I went in thinking I was on top of this, and I presented some well-thought-out plans but came away feeling I missed the mark completely!"

She couldn't comprehend why she bombed in her interview until the next day when her boss's boss called her into his office and said, "I can see that you know your stuff, but you don't just come into a meeting and tell me what to do!"

Michelle was mortified. "I lost the trust of my boss's boss. My intention was to show both of them that I was ready to step up and accept the responsibilities of the new position."

It's perfectly fine to offer solutions, but Michelle should have first understood what the two men's priorities were, reiterated their objectives to show that she acknowledges and aligns with their goals, then presented her solutions as ways that would help the two men achieve those goals.

"I'M REALLY NOT LOOKING TO BE IMPROVED UPON."

Achieving goals is very important to a man. It's his best way of proving his competence, and it makes him feel good about himself and his abilities. For him to feel good about himself, a man is driven to achieving his goals on his own. Someone else can't achieve them for him. To a man, working independently is his display of efficiency, power, and competence.

Understanding this male characteristic can help women understand why men resist being corrected or being told what to do. To offer a man unsolicited advice is to presume that he doesn't know what to do or that he can't do it on his own.

Again, men don't commonly share their feelings, but in our workshops, this is how they express their need for independence and acceptance:

- "Please don't try to change me or correct me."
- "Value me for who and what I am. I'm not looking to be improved upon!"
- "I know what needs to be done and I can do it."

Women have to be very careful about seeking to improve a man when he hasn't asked for that kind of input. If he gives her the opportunity to do that, then it's fine. But a woman looking to establish trust should be aware that she's beginning to walk on thin ice if she sounds too critical and offers more advice than was asked or expected.

Women have a tendency to want to improve things, even if they're working well. There's this ongoing belief that "things can always be improved." Men see their world differently. They tend to believe that "if it's not broke, don't fix it." Carry this view to the workplace and we can see why many women who enter management positions often feel an automatic responsibility to give direction to other people's work. While some women tend to be more open to this level of involvement and collaboration, this approach easily loses the trust of the men around her.

A woman can build her credibility with a man by first seeing the good in him and his efforts and supporting, instead of correcting, those efforts. When a man feels that a woman is not trying to improve him, he is much more likely to seek her out for her ideas and go to her often for feedback and advice.

BLEND QUESTIONS WITH ACTION

During workshops, when we explore the challenges men and women face in working together, some men state that their biggest difficulty is that women tend to ask too many questions, especially during meetings when, they feel, questions tend to slow progress on action items and delay decision making.

Women commonly agree that they do ask more questions than men, but they believe that their questions are their best contributions, intended to encourage collaboration, discover what's important, and arrive at a best possible outcome.

The challenge for women is in not asking fewer questions, but discovering how to frame their questions in ways that connect better with men. In each of these examples, a woman could help a man to get the right message and to offer his support immediately simply by adding a positive, upbeat comment before the question, or by making a clear and direct request.

Indirect questions tend to challenge	Being more direct lends credibility
"How can you be serious?"	"That amazes me! How can that be true?"
"What makes you think that will work?"	"You have a good idea there, but I'd like to know your thoughts on implementing it."
"But, what does everyone else think?"	"We have to get to a decision, but let's confirm we have everyone's buy-in first."
"Is this the best direction the company can take?"	"That will achieve our goal, but I think there's a way we can arrive there more effectively."

Women and men bring different viewpoints and experiences to the table, and when they work together, they add a richer collection of perspectives to the decision-making process. And it's not a matter of having equal numbers of men and women on teams; it's having a team comprised of members who have enough gender intelligence to understand and value what women and men have to contribute in their own unique ways.

DON'T ASSUME INSENSITIVITY

Men understand, more than ever, that successful leadership requires becoming more perceptive of their environment and mindful of the needs, motivations, and interests of the people around them. Nevertheless, being sensitive is not a natural and effortless response for men.

A man's general nature is to think about things silently before sharing what's on his mind. Internally and quietly, he may be figuring out the most correct or useful response. He could be reacting this way while alone, in a one-to-one conversation with someone, or while sitting in a noisy room full of people. This is most confusing and often frustrating to women.

If a man doesn't have enough information to respond, or her question or comment falls outside of his linear thinking process, he may not say anything at all or very little. It gives a woman the impression that he's not listening, isn't interested in what she's saying, or doesn't care. A gender-intelligent woman will be more understanding when a man appears to be indifferent, self-absorbed, or noncollaborative. She appreciates that it's likely not personal or intentional on his part but simply preoccupation with thoughts of his own.

Here are some examples of how a gender-intelligent woman can express her support when a man is under stress and appears inattentive or disengaged. Some of these suggestions may not be reactions that all men can relate to, but the majority of men will. Also keep in mind that, just as men earn the trust of women by stepping outside their own comfort zone, women can earn the trust of men by stepping outside theirs.

- When making a suggestion or presenting a proposal or plan of action, women might consider getting to the point and avoid talking about problems first. Focus more on what you think should be done or what the results will be.

- Consider being direct when making a request. Don't talk about a problem and wait for him to offer his support. When women are not direct, men often feel manipulated. The less a man feels obliged to do something, the more willing he may be to help.

- Consider taking credit for your achievements, and when taking credit, focus on what results you achieved instead of talking about how hard you worked.

- Consider avoiding noticing and pointing out his fatigue or stress level by saying in a sympathetic tone, "You look tired," or "What's wrong?" Worrying or showing concern about him may weaken him further, and he'll tend to find it offensive. A more relaxed response demonstrates a level of trust that says, "I'm sure you can handle it."

- Minimize his mistakes or his forgetfulness. When a man makes a mistake and a woman doesn't make a big deal out of it, he tends to feel greater trust in her and belief in himself.
- Say no graciously. A man is typically turned off when a woman uses how much she has to do as a way of saying no. From his perspective, a simple "I can't do it" is often enough. If he wants to know more, he'll often ask.

By being more direct in her interactions and framing her conversations in ways to ensure her male coworkers are more aware of her meaning, needs, and expectations, women tend to induce more trust from men. He, in turn, will show greater appreciation for her acceptance of him and for not taking offense at what may appear to be inattentiveness or unconcern. He'll often return her understanding by demonstrating trust in her and expressing greater interest in cooperating and collaborating with her.

THE PERSONAL SIDE OF LIFE: A CIRCLE OF TRUST

WHAT WOMEN WANT

For Sarah, it's the little things that her husband, Jim, does each day that show he cares. After 25 years of marriage, those little things demonstrate to Sarah that his love for her hasn't waned. To hear Sarah tell it, you would think that she and her husband are newlyweds.

"Every morning as I'm getting ready for work, and before Jim sets off for the office, he brings the newspaper into the house and makes coffee for us. He's an early bird, so he's always on his way before the sun is up. In the winter, he times it so water is boiling and ready for me because he knows oatmeal gets me started on cold mornings. And in the summer, there's always a half glass of orange juice waiting for me on the kitchen island along with half his doughnut. It's a sharing thing he started years ago and is still really cute to me.

"It may not seem like a lot, but these are little things he does for me that tell me I'm always on his mind, that he's always considering me. If he gets home first, he'll start dinner. I can't recall once during our entire marriage when I came home and there wasn't something thawing on the counter, cooking on the range, or takeout warming in the oven.

"When our children were younger, he used to use lunch breaks to help out with transporting them to their doctor's appointments, and one of us would always be at the after-school events. It was never just me alone. We had our share of tough times, but I never lost my trust in him, and I let him know it every day."

To women, words don't matter nearly as much as actions. The little things make a difference—the subtle things a husband does for his wife truly count—and they remind her how much he cares for her. It's not hard work for a man, or at least it shouldn't be. It's an honest excitement and desire on his part to want to give, and to continue to give. A man needs to understand that if he consistently treats the woman he loves as someone he values, he will be astounded at how quickly trust will grow—and, along with it, his relationship with her.

WHAT MEN WANT

At work, a man's tendency is to place trust in a woman he feels is capable and confident, someone who will support him and help him achieve his goals. In his personal life, a man's feeling of being supported is just as important. Moreover, a man commonly thrives when he knows that his partner trusts him, appreciates what he does, admires him for his uniqueness, and believes in his abilities.

When a woman's attitude is open and receptive toward a man, he feels trusted. To trust a man is to believe that he is doing his best and that he wants the best for his partner. When a woman's reactions reveal a positive belief in her man's abilities and intentions, his primary love need is fulfilled. Automatically, he is more caring and attentive to her feelings and needs.

When a woman acknowledges having received personal benefit and value from a man's efforts, he feels appreciated. When a man feels appreciated, he knows his effort is not wasted and is encouraged and motivated to give more.

Just as a woman needs to feel a man's devotion, a man has a primary need to feel a woman's admiration. A man feels admired when she is happily amazed by his unique characteristics or talents, which may include humor, strength, persistence, integrity, honesty, romance, kindness, and other virtues many today consider old-fashioned—but truly are not. When a man feels admired, he feels secure enough to devote himself to his woman and adore her.

When a woman's attitude expresses trust, appreciation, and admiration, it encourages a man to be all that he can be. And feeling encouraged and believed in motivates him to give her the loving re assurance that she needs. She, then, is encouraged to extend her trust in him. It's a full circle that positively feeds on itself: she needs devotion, and the more she admires her man, the greater devotion he gives her in return.

ELEVEN

BRIDGING OUR DIFFERENT VALUES

WHAT WE VALUE IN OUR WORLD AND WHAT WE VALUE MOST IN others defines what we value most in ourselves. What we treasure and consider important shapes us and influences how we view the world and our place in it. It guides us in how we approach situations and relate to others. Living by their values gives both men and women the greatest sense of personal fulfillment and success.

Men and women often find themselves at opposite ends of the spectrum when it comes to what they value at work, how they prefer to work, what they expect of others, and what they expect of themselves. This is reflected in these statements:

- "Your belief in me means everything."
- "I appreciate your listening."
- "Everyone should be heard."
- "In the end, it's the results that matter."
- "If we encourage the effort, we improve the results."
- "I believe in strong, decisive leadership."
- "The best leaders share in their leadership."

Women most value building alliances, developing relationships, and collaborating toward a common goal while improving processes and people along the way. Women value sharing their leadership and decision making, and ensuring everyone is involved. Women place value on improving performance and maximizing productivity.

Men most value achieving results, from their own efforts and that of others. Men value independent work, and when on a team, getting each individual to work as effectively and efficiently as possible toward a shared goal, doing the right and necessary things in the shortest amount of time. They're comfortable working in hierarchies and often declare their leadership. Men place value on alignment, momentum, and results.

GENDER FACTS[1]

- 74 percent of women value experiencing the journey as much as achieving the results.
- 85 percent of men put a greater value on achieving the results and beating the competition than on experiencing the journey itself.

Men's values, for generations, have defined the rules of engagement in the workplace. Since the late 1940s, in the aftermath of World War Two, the military model of duty, command, and leadership and many of the methods so successful in managing personnel and logistics on different continents carried over into private practice. That command-and-control model still undergirds many of the business practices and cultures of corporations, organizations, and even educational institutions.

Women have represented half the workforce since the 1980s. Yet the values that men practice and are most comfortable with continue to define most all the rules, practices, and procedures at work, often placing men and women at odds with what the other gender values. Change is slow, but men are gradually adopting new practices to respond to an increasingly complex and diverse marketplace, and they recognize that half their workforce often aligns with and performs to a completely different set of values, needs, and expectations than men.

The blind spot preventing change is men's and women's inability to understand what's most valued by the other gender and why. Remove the blind spot and men and women are able to discover ways to bridge their different values in the workplace and allow both genders to maintain their authenticity yet complement each other's.

"VALUES DON'T MATTER IF WE'RE NOT MAKING THE NUMBERS "

The CEO takes center stage on the first day of the annual sales conference. Within the first five minutes of his speech he proclaims, "I'm so glad that all our employees aspire to our values of collaboration and inclusiveness, but these values won't matter if we're not making the numbers!"

The men in the audience nod understandingly: "He's right. We have to buckle down and get it done." . . . "We've got ninety days to make a difference. We have to move faster on some of our decisions if we want to make our numbers."

The women have a completely different take: "What? Did he just say what I thought I heard him say? These values are not just lip service, they're *what* women value. It's why I'm here!" . . . "Everyone participating motivates me and improves our productivity. I'm not about quick decisions and success at any cost."

A gender-intelligent CEO would have opened differently: "We need to work harder at being inclusive and bringing our best ideas together. Our values improve our productivity and performance, and inspire us to achieve our results."

MAPPING THE DISTANCE

Women and men often lie on different ends of a continuum when it comes to what each gender values. Understanding what she or he is thinking and why is the only way we can begin to appreciate each other and to take steps closer to each other's way of working.

What men tend to value most in the workplace are power, competence, efficiency, action, and accomplishment. A man will often undertake tasks to prove his ability and worth, to feel competent and confident, and to develop his knowledge and skills. His sense of self and success is in his ability to set and achieve objectives.

While women value achievement, generally more important to them are the values of support, trust, and communication. Their interests are in the presence and quality of working relations and collaborative, networked environments. And their sense of self and success is in sharing and cooperating in the process of achieving their objectives.

Here are the four value spectrums that most distinguish women from men. While these value orientations may be found in many women and many men, they are not necessarily found in all women or all men.

Value Spectrum	Women's Inclination	Men's Inclination
Improve versus Maintain	"Anything can be improved and made to work better."	"If it's not broken, don't fix it."
Together versus Independently	"I come up with more ideas when I'm working with others."	"I come up with my best ideas when I can concentrate alone."
Journey versus Results	"Our efforts together matter as much as our results."	"Winning matters most."
Sharing versus Declaring	"Everyone should contribute to the decision."	"A leader leads. I'm expected to make decisions."

These may be the four value spectrums that distinguish how women and men approach work, engage with others, and lead, but it doesn't have to be one side "versus" the other. There are many ways in which men and women are finding common ground and bridging their differences in the workplace. It begins with understanding where the other gender places his or her greatest value and importance, and why.

<u>IMPROVE</u>———————<u>MAINTAIN</u>

Women tend to believe that when something is working, it can most likely work better. Women often feel compelled to improve on their environment and the people who interact with them.

Creating change is second nature to women in part because it is a natural activity in their lives. For women, it's a sign of caring to give advice and suggestions. When they care about someone or something, such as having passion for a project, product, or client, they freely point out what can be improved and suggest how to do it. To women, offering advice and constructive criticism is giving their best at work.

Seeking continuous improvement doesn't always work in a woman's favor though. To offer a man unsolicited advice or to recommend "areas of improvement" implies that he's incapable of thinking through an issue and accomplishing a task on his own. When a woman tries to change or improve her male coworker or his work effort, his immediate interpretation is that he's made a mistake or he's somehow defective. He'll tend to feel unappreciated, become self-defending, and will often resist being corrected or told what to do.

A woman's sometimes-endless pursuit of improvement to get something just right can cause her to fall into an improvement cycle trap—a perfection trap—in which overpreparation always succeeds in driving up her stress levels but not necessarily improving her work product.

At a recent keynote address to women executives in the financial services industry, I asked, "How many of you believe you overprepare for meetings? How many of you have difficulty in knowing and accepting when 'good enough is good enough'?" Every hand in the room shot up.

Women often find themselves in the weeds because of their impulse to overthink an issue, improve a report, write an article, or perfect a speech. It's true that everything can always be improved upon, but women have to be rigorous with themselves to maintain forward momentum. In workshops, women often share that they wish they could disengage as quickly and completely as men do, leave well enough alone, and move on to another issue and another decision.

Men are indeed on the other end of this spectrum! If something is working, their tendency is not to waste time looking to improve what's not broken. Their motto: "Just leave it alone if it's working."

While there's commonly a drive in women to improve things, there's often a desire in men to achieve more with what's already there. It's not that men want more of the same or are unchanging in their nature. It's just the opposite. Men want growth and results, but they'll only feel compelled to change something when that something stops functioning.

This underlies the male principle of "efficiency." Men tend to want to do something right or fix something correctly the first time so they don't have to fix it again—ever, if possible! They often want to get the maximum utility out of anything before replacing or improving on it. Men will adapt to change, but only if it's necessary and proven to be more effective than what they're already doing.

THE IKEA STORY

IKEA was founded in 1943 by teenager Ingvar Kamprad who at first sold small items (wallets, keychains, pens) mostly produced in Sweden at low prices. Five years later, after advertising and building his enterprise into a makeshift mail-order business, he introduced locally produced furniture, and then published his first catalog in 1951. In 1953 he opened his first showroom, and three years later started the self-assembly, flat-pack concept to ship his furniture. For two decades, IKEA's primary business model was to sell furniture from catalogs. After placing their orders, customers would receive flat boxes efficiently filled with disassembled furniture along with detailed instructions. In 1965, Kamprad opened his first self-serve warehouse. IKEA had developed a very successful business concept based on Kamprad's vision of effectively and efficiently warehousing and shipping low-cost furniture and household goods in a way that avoided "transporting and storing air." Over the next 20 years, Kamprad spread his vision, establishing stores first in Europe and in Canada.[2]

In 1985, the first IKEA store in the United States opened in Philadelphia, Pennsylvania, and women leaders at IKEA headquarters in Leiden, Netherlands, were tasked with creating a different experience for this new market. Statistics showed that women in the United States made 90 percent of the purchase decisions for furniture and were not inclined to base their buying decision on pictures in a catalog.

IKEA's management believed that woman shoppers should be able to experience what the furniture would look like when completely assembled—whether a living room, kitchen, bedroom, or child's room. They decided to create rooms within their stores in the United States and other countries that would embody a "what would it look like if I lived there" perspective. Fine touches were added with wall art, pillows, furniture, etc. Men loved the rooms idea as well. It's far easier to follow assembly instructions and determine the amount of space needed for the furniture item after seeing the fully assembled product.

IKEA is the perfect example of packaged efficiency created by men and the added experience of women looking to improve on an already great concept. IKEA sales skyrocketed well beyond expectations, and the company is now the world's largest furniture retailer. It's a perfect example of gender intelligence in action—men and women bridging their values to create a better product.

TOGETHER————————INDEPENDENTLY

Women commonly have a natural facility in recognizing patterns of connections among people, ideas, processes, and communities. It inspires them to create alliances, to see the interrelationship of people and things, and to expand those relationships. It intuitively encourages women to work and collaborate with others.

Men tend not to be that relational. A man's inclination is to work alone when solving problems, and he'll do fine in his solitude as long as he's productive. He'll immerse himself, shut out the outside world, and complete the task. If the issue is too complicated for him to handle alone, he'll get others involved, though certain rules will still apply.

A man tends to approach teamwork as an individual working with other individuals rather than as a team member "becoming one" with the team. He'll maintain his sense of independence and self-determination and ensure that his role and what's expected of him is defined and unambiguous. If a man is identified and valued this way—as an individual—he'll know that he's an asset and bring his best work to the team.

The tendency for a man is to think about what he needs to do to achieve his goal so that the team will succeed. He's doesn't concern himself with what other team members are doing unless their actions impact his success. His sense of achievement is dependent upon his personal results.

A woman's tendency will be to focus on what the team needs, what others require in order for the team to succeed—a bigger, more improved "WE." If the team is not getting what it needs, she's going to stay overtime out of a sense of responsibility—or, often, out of a sense of guilt. She'll see to everyone's needs before she'll attend to her own. Her sense of achievement is dependent on the success of the team.

"IF IT MAKES YOU HAPPY."

Judy, a veteran of Wall Street and motherhood with two teenage children, is having lunch with Margaret, a younger, single woman just starting out with the investment firm.

Margaret opens up before even touching her salad: "Who came up with the idea that single women don't have a life? I envy you, Judy. I want to meet someone special and have children early, so they can be self-sufficient like yours are and I can go back to pursuing my career while I'm still young. The money's great, but I'm putting in 12-hour days and working weekends. Today is the first chance we've had to have lunch together in I can't remember how long. I don't know how you did it then or how you're doing it now."

Judy pauses before responding, not wanting to stress Margaret out even further, but she feels a need to share her experience. "I feel for you Margaret, but here's a thought for you: single women may carry the burden of workload, but working mothers carry the burden of guilt."

Margaret asks, "I agree with the burden, but what do *you* feel guilty about?"

"The same thing that makes you feel guilty when you take an afternoon off for personal reasons: not being there to share the team's burden, especially on weekends. I know the team still puts in weekends. My kids may get off to school in the morning and are doing homework when I get home, but they still need me, especially on weekends—when you're here working! But I'm learning to come to terms with myself and fight this feeling of guilt."

"What about Scott?" Margaret asks. "Doesn't he help?"

"Sure he does. Scott's a great dad and loving husband, but you're going to find out that men generally don't see the world and their place in it the same way we do. Try as they might, they're not as empathetic as women or feel the same sense of responsibility for others. It's not their fault. It's just the way they're built. . . .

"Scott works at it though. He gets things done and cares about me, but *I* carry the burden of guilt when I'm at the office, thinking of my family. And I feel guilty when I'm home, thinking of the office. Scott can turn it off—better than I can—when he walks through the door. He's learning to be like me and I'm learning to be like him!"

"But right now," Margaret says, "I don't see ever having children, let alone meeting someone significant."

"Look, Margaret, the firm is never going to encourage you to take time off and have children. They'll offer you flexibility, but *you* have to make the time. You're talented and ambitious, and this company will bend over backward to keep you. If not, other companies will want you. Fight the guilt. You can have it all—you just don't need to do it all at once. If this is what you desire, if it makes you happy, do it!"

This values continuum of "caring for others" on the one end and "caring for self" on the other influences aspects of women's and men's careers, such as negotiation. Men and women approach negotiation differently, primarily because they view the relational aspects of the negotiation differently. In a study, men and women were asked whether negotiation is like a poker game, dance, bullfight, or tennis match. Men were most likely to say "poker game," while women most often described negotiation as a "dance," which implies that women see it as a collaboration rather than an activity in which there's a winner and a loser.[3]

The same study shows that it doesn't help women to act more like men when negotiating. It's not that women don't make great poker players, it's just that when they're negotiating, they tend to personalize their request for greater compensation or more resources, which comes across as a complaint or being upset. A woman also tends to apologize or talk about "feelings" when she's negotiating: "I'm sorry

THE SCIENCE SIDE

In chapter three, we described how the inferior parietal lobule (IPL) is the part of the brain that receives signals representing the sensation of touch, self-perception, and vision, and integrates these signals in such a way that enables an individual to determine self-identity, direction, and meaning. It could be said that, in large part, the IPL influences where, when, and how men and women place the importance in their lives and express their values.

The IPL tends to be larger on the left—or logical, analytical, and objective—side of the brain in men,[4] continuously prompting them to taking action, and with a fixed focus on task and achievement. Men tend to gauge their ability and measure their worth by their accomplishments and results. They feel great comfort and competence when solving problems in isolation and thinking things through to their logical conclusions.

Being so goal-driven, a man will often zero in on the most effective and efficient way of getting from point A to point B, what the outcome will be as a result of his efforts, and if that outcome is worth achieving.

In women, the IPL is commonly larger on the right—or intuitive, thoughtful, and subjective—side of the brain, and while men tend to use only one side of their brain at a time, women tend to use both cerebral areas at once, given them a more enhanced visual, verbal, and emotional connection with others. Women tend to be better at sensing emotional messages in conversations, gestures, and facial expressions.[5]

A woman's priority is not so much finding the most efficient path to accomplishing a task as it is building relationships that support collaboration. Women are inclined to measure themselves by their successes in establishing alliances, developing people and relationships, and sharing knowledge.[6]

Our gender differences are not black and white, and there are exceptions to every rule. It is easy to find women who prefer to think and work alone and focus more on results and less on relations. It's easy to find men who have their best ideas when collaborating and are more inclusive in their leadership.

What's valuable and adds a depth of perception and richness to our perspective is the understanding of our own general nature, the general nature of the other gender, and what compels most men and women to think and act as they do.

to ask for this, but I feel that I deserve a raise," or "I think I'm worth it," or "Look at all that I've done." Statements such as these lessen her credibility and the weight of her argument.

All of this changes, though, when women negotiate on behalf of others. When negotiating for others—whether for her department, her team, or for a cause—a woman's confidence and performance increases over that of a man's.[7] This is, at times, self-defeating for a woman as she'll tend to overvalue relationships and undervalue herself.

Alternatively, a gender-intelligent woman is still a strong negotiator for others, but practices more self-care by approaching personal negotiation with the mindset that she and the company will benefit from the outcome. She externalizes the reasons for higher personal compensation or greater resources by citing her accomplishments and achievements as well as her future value to the organization. This is reasoning male negotiators understand and more readily align with, especially the focus on future value and performance.

JOURNEY————————RESULTS

Women tend to thrive on collaboration, cooperation, communication, and mutual support. They care about the results, but they gain just as much if not more sense of purpose and satisfaction when confronting and resolving challenges along the way.

Women tend to go about accomplishing their objectives by building relationships first, then improving those relationships in the attainment of their goals. With such statements as, "We're accomplishing some great things together," or, "Thank you for recognizing my effort," or, "I really enjoy working with you!" a woman shares and relates with others, expressing her fulfillment in the journey undertaken together. Accomplishing the journey as a team validates her efforts and gives her work meaning.

Men tend to approach work and engage others in a different way. A man's inclination is to find the shortest distance between two points and move along that course as effectively as possible, by doing the right and necessary things in order of importance. He'll then work as efficiently as possible, by doing those right things in the shortest amount of time and with the least amount of resources.

At a recent workshop, a senior male executive summed it up this way: "I feel accomplishment and relief only when things are completed. I'll develop a tunnel vision around what's expected of me and my team right through to the results. I see and hear things around me but filter them down or out. Some days, I couldn't tell you who was in the office or who I even had lunch with!"

A man's personal fulfillment comes at the end of the journey when he can see the results of his efforts and be recognized and appreciated for his performance. While a woman will more likely welcome the process and finds value in the effort, a man will endure the process and place greater value on the results. Thus, a man will likely say to team members, "I don't care how you do it, I trust you. Just get it done!" Or, "We either win or lose." Or, "We reached our goal, now let's do it again next year." Being goal-driven is a natural, wired-in capacity in men, and hugely complementary to a woman's inclination to build alliances, develop strong relations, and improve the capacity of people and processes networked along the way.

Women tend to believe that their attention to the process and to the people engaged in the task builds strong teams and creates environments that breed success. This is why women place such high value on the journey: to uncover, embrace, and improve that integrity between the means and ends.

A man tends not to show the same level of awareness or concern for the issues surrounding the efforts and needs of others until it affects his ability to achieve the results. A man won't normally get involved in the personalities, emotions, or situations of his coworkers. It doesn't necessarily mean he isn't observant or caring. His nature is to take in less, focus only on those things directly related to the objective, and do all this with far less concern for details. But focusing only on the results doesn't often improve and seldom sustains the effectiveness of a team.

"IT WASN'T JUST FOR THE MONEY."

A veteran sales representative walks into her sales manager's office and resigns. The manager is shocked, too shocked to ask her why she's quitting. He becomes increasingly upset that she would leave him in a lurch this way and is at a total loss for words. He freezes for what seems like seconds to him but hours to her, confirming her feelings and experiences, "He doesn't even care to ask me why."

During her post-exit interview, she tells the human resources head that she's resigning because she found a new job that pays more with better benefits. HR goes to senior leadership and says, "We may need to review our pay and benefits packages if we want to retain our key employees."

Three months later, the senior leadership calls an emergency staff meeting with the vice president of sales to find out why three of their best reps, two women and one man, simply quit. "We're now paying more in salary and commission than our competition, but we're still losing people. We can't afford to lose clients because of this."

Six months later, in a post-exit interview, the sales rep who quit for a better job and pay tells me, "It wasn't just for the money, although that's what I told them. I'm making less actually. I like the culture of this new company. I feel part of a team here. They like my ideas and regularly ask me my opinion. The workload's the same, and we're just as competitive, but not with each other! I feel like we're pulling together. It may sound silly, but people seem to care more about each other here. I think our prospects pick that up during sales presentations too."

SHARE——————————DECLARE

In chapter one, we talked about an extensive global study conducted by McKinsey & Company that revealed the different though complementary leadership strengths of men and women. Of the nine traits cited, men and women equally apply intellectual stimulation and effective communication. More often than men, women apply people development and participative decision making. And more often than women, men apply individual decision making and control and corrective action. McKinsey defines control and corrective action as performance management: "Monitoring individuals' performance including shortfalls against goals and taking corrective action when needed."[8] For men, performance management ensures the results, and the style of leadership that ensures performance is hierarchal, organized, and directed.

People development is on the opposite end of the continuum of strengths, being women's most distinctive leadership trait. McKinsey defines people development as "building a team atmosphere in which everyone is encouraged to participate in decision making."

We distinguish what women and men value and personify in their leadership as Sharing in leadership and Declaring in leadership.

Sharing may be exemplified by these statements: "I won't make a critical decision without balanced input from the men and women on my staff," or "I trust you to make the best decision for your region," or "I'd like your thoughts before we move forward."

Declaring may be exemplified by these statements: "Our global launch *will* take place on the first of the month," or "I'll convince the board that we belong in those markets," or "My decision was final."

"THE BEST IS BOTH."

A woman CEO of a large global company told me recently how she defines her leadership. "I share my leadership with others. By that I mean, I place trust in the hands of others to make decisions. We're a global company and I recognize that I can't be everywhere at once. So I have a network of leaders around the world that I can fully depend upon. We talk weekly, but they have their autonomy. Two-thirds of my regional leaders are men and they thrive in that independence.

"It wasn't always this way here. I struggled for over 20 years, climbing the ladder in a corporate world built around men's values. Every leadership training course I took was designed for the men in the room, not me. For two years, I was the only woman on the executive team. You can imagine how a woman in that environment can start to pick up and mimic men's traits. It's like being around all brothers all the time!

"I define my leadership as one of sharing and caring. It's all about people development and involvement. I may have compromised my values in the past to get here, but I don't compromise my values any longer. But I did develop an understanding of how and why men lead as they do and why people follow. I believe strong directive leadership has its place to ensure performance goals are attained, but the healthiest environment for that form of leadership must be one of collaboration. With more than half my staff being male, the best is both forms of leadership—sharing *and* declaring."

By incorporating a bit of a male mindset in their leadership, women can avoid a big issue that tends to hold them back. The value women place on relationships can enhance their ability to work with others and encourage, motivate, develop, and inspire their team members. However, that orientation also presents a key developmental challenge for women who can become consumed in the connectivity and, as we discovered in an earlier story, consumed in guilt. The challenge for women is to develop a sense of boundaries to workplace relations as men do and to practice more focus on self-care.

Since the 1980s, shifts have occurred away from an exclusively male paradigm of leadership to a more decentralized and participative model. Much of this change has been driven by the complexity and speed of global business and need for companies to make quick and informed decisions, sometimes worlds apart. But change is slow, even for global companies whose workforces are comprised of as many women as men and who have customers who are virtually all women.

Female leaders	Male leaders
Define their leadership in the strength and power of their networks.	Define their leadership through their accomplishments and the results of others.
Are aware of the specific situations and needs of individuals and groups and how those issues can affect the organization.	Are more attentive at the macro level—the financial and operational needs of the organization—and not as concerned at the individual level.
Decentralize planning and share decision making.	Centralize planning with performance measures and hierarchial decision making.
Directly empathize, encourage, and praise others. Seek to resolve emotional conflicts through communication: "Let's talk about it."	Promote independent resolution of problems and control emotional vulnerability: "Less feeling, more doing!"

So, how would you build the future paradigm of leadership? Many books have been written about an eventual trend toward participative leadership, and there's a high level of buy-in by business and government leaders that this is where we are going—where we *have* to go!

The reality is that there's value on both sides of the leadership spectrum—a centerpoint of leadership that incorporates the best of what women and men bring to the table. Organizations that have a greater balance of women and men in leadership are discovering one another's value points and accelerating toward the sharing of leadership.

THE PERSONAL SIDE OF LIFE

Margaret walks into Grand Central Station and catches the last train to her modest home in New Rochelle. Sitting there alone in the near-empty car, she has time to think about what Judy said at lunch earlier today—about feeling guilty for not working weekends. Then it dawns on Margaret: "Is my sense of guilt the reason Larry and I are not dating as much as we used to?"

Margaret and Larry have been seeing each other for eight months. She met him at the hospital where she volunteers once or twice a month and found Larry to be someone she could really connect with, someone different from the men in her office.

Since they started dating, every weekend when Margaret doesn't have to be in midtown working she's calling or texting Larry, suggesting things they can do. But lately, Larry has become increasingly irritable, passive, and moody when they are together.

She slowly realizes, "I feel guilty those times that I had to work when he wanted to drive to the mountains for the weekend, and now I think I'm overcompensating when I'm free. I just want to spend as much time with him as I can to see if he's really the one and to let him know that I'm really interested in him."

The closer Margaret's train gets to her stop, the more flooded her thoughts are of her personal life and the more distant her concerns for the unrelenting workload at the office and her teammates. "We're not intimate anymore. He used to be so charming and romantic. I think it's over."

But it doesn't have to be over. Margaret's feelings of guilt and seeking forgiveness by overcompensating when they are together are what's causing Larry to pull away. Moreover, she's pushing him away by resenting him for not being responsive when they are together.

Margaret needs to not worry about Larry so much and start taking better care of herself and her own needs and interests. By doing things she wants to do, she'll express less guilt, let go of her resentment toward Larry, and make her happiness less dependent on his happiness—an attitude that is most likely currently smothering him.

Each day trains, cars, and airplanes are filled with millions of single and married women and men, all looking for some sort of balance between their working lives and their personal lives, when what they really desire is greater harmony between those two worlds.

TWELVE

ACHIEVING
WORK-PERSONAL
LIFE HARMONY

THROUGHOUT THIS BOOK, WE'VE EXPLORED THE CHALLENGES and opportunities faced by men and women as they strive to understand each other better and find personal success in their work lives and personal lives. Complicating that challenge is the reality that these two lives are not as separate and clearly designated as they were just a generation ago.

Our heightened level of stress and fatigue at work and at home is the result of our failed attempts to balance the limited time and dwindling energy that we have between these two worlds. Given the complexity and constancy of global business and advances in technology, a 9-to-5 workday or a management position that allows you to leave work at the office rarely exists anymore.

There's another dynamic at play! Since the year 2000, 80 percent of the workforce has been comprised of dual-earner couples, a huge difference from 1980 when it was 25 percent, and from 1950 when it was virtually unheard of. This trend is not abating, nor is it limited to the United States or Europe. A dual-income household is, today, a global societal norm.[1]

GENDER FACTS[2]

- 91 percent of women and 94 percent of men agree that they would want to be more flexible with their schedules.
- Yet only 15 percent of women and 20 percent of men feel flexible work arrangements would not jeopardize their career advancement.

Perhaps no other phenomenon has had a greater effect on society, altering the way men and women interact and how families live and spend their time. Today, the greatest challenge facing men and women is how to juggle their jobs and family responsibilities so that everyone feels appreciated and fulfilled.

There are few differences between how men and women view work- versus personal-life balance. Of course, women balance many more roles, but feeling the pressure of the workload and the loss of personal time is equally felt by both genders.

COMPETING LIVES

Work life–personal life balance suggests people must live two separate lives—one at work and one anywhere but work. Yet the separation between these two lives is not that clean. Men and women are carrying unresolved personal problems and family issues to work ("I have to call the school and let them know my child is home sick today"), and they bring work-related responsibilities and deadlines home ("Maybe I can get a couple more hours in after dinner").

We've discovered in our workshops over the years that, regardless of country, women and men describe the lack of balance differently: women feel they have too little time for daily life activities while men feel the endless pressure to perform and deliver.

Women say:

- "When I'm at work, I think about home, and when I'm home, I think about work."

- "I'm too tired after work to do household chores."
- "I feel guilty leaving at 5 P.M. sharp every day."

Men say:
- "It seems I'm always at work, even when I'm at home."
- "There's no time anymore for hobbies or my own interests."
- "I just can't leave the office for a family commitment!"

The phrase "work life–personal life balance" suggests a need to create time equality between two competing lives, as if the possibility of finding an optimal distribution of time between both lives can be found. This is a near-impossible task, particularly for women. Women tend not to separate and sequence their thoughts as easily as men do. A great source of stress for women comes from having to juggle many competing ideas and agendas at once, giving them the feeling of never having enough time for anything, and often a sense of guilt for being unable to devote enough time whether at work or at home.

Men can typically separate and isolate competing thoughts to focus on one issue at a time more easily than women can. For men, the problem is that the pressure to perform has created an endless imbalance in their lives: an almost singular focus on work. The source of stress for men often comes from having to sacrifice their personal lives, work long hours, and deliver results.

Women and men can never fully achieve work-personal life balance and are setting themselves up for disappointment every time they try. Leading two separate lives with each competing for a fixed amount of time is not the solution.

CONGRUOUS LIVES

Work-personal life balance becomes a preoccupation with finding and maintaining an equilibrium at all times. This quest often becomes the pursuit of finding balance itself instead of focusing on what's being balanced. The only thing that ends up being equally distributed is stress and anxiety, and a feeling of constantly "coming up short" at work and at home.

To seek work-personal life *harmony*, on the other hand, is to accept and embrace both worlds as one, not to seek separation but rather a more orchestrated congruity between one's work life and personal life. Work-personal life harmony focuses on energy rather than time— living fully in moments as they occur rather than measuring the time allotted to each moment.

For many men and women, work-personal life harmony means pursuing a career that agrees with one's personal life. But that's not always possible. Many men and women don't have a choice in their careers. Many are stuck in their jobs or are not satisfied with the career track they're currently on. But that doesn't mean they shouldn't try to attain their own coexistence and place of calm—regardless of what their work is or where it takes them.

Women, in particular, suffer most from a scarcity of time and need to be more self-initiating in defining the boundaries of their working life and the time devoted to it. They'll join companies committed to having work flexibility programs, but they can't expect the company to encourage their participation.

Women have to move away from the guilt feelings described in the previous chapter and take the initiative to practice greater self-care. Gender-intelligent companies and attentive leaders are realizing that empowering a woman with flexibility and time relieves her stress and inspires her to contribute even more.

"GIVE ME FRIDAYS AND I'LL GIVE YOU 200 PERCENT!"

During a workshop segment on negotiation, a woman shared her experience in high-tech sales before her promotion to senior management. She was the only woman on the sales team at the time but "worked hard to prove that I could sell just as well as the guys in the department!" She consistently attained 125 to 150 percent of her sales quotas, regardless of what her quotas were set at.

"Our home life was thrown into a tailspin when my husband's mother took ill and had to move in with us. She couldn't live alone anymore, and we weren't about to put her in a nursing home—not after all she had done for us over the years.

"Peter and I ran the numbers, and we realized that we couldn't afford the cost of home care five days a week. I also wanted to ensure a quality of life for Grace's remaining years. Peter was hoping he could be the one to spend more time at home, but the nature of his work and travel schedule just wouldn't allow it.

"I had no choice but to confront my boss and make him an offer I prayed he wouldn't refuse. I told him I needed Fridays off, and in return I would deliver 200 percent of my sales quota instead of my usual 150. I also promised him that if I ever fell off that 200 percent mark, I would work Fridays again. I know I surprised him, but he agreed in the end. I think he appreciated the fact that I gave him a solution and not just a problem.

"For three years, I delivered 200 percent or more of my quota and was one of the hardest-working sale reps on the team. I accomplished more in four days than others were pulling off in five! When I was at work, I worked hard, and when I was home, I was home 100 percent!

"Grace is still with us and though I'm in senior management now, I still work out of my home on Fridays. I won't compromise that symmetry that I've created between my work and my personal life."

As we noted several times in our book, women have a natural capacity to multithink and multitask, but this innate talent can be just as much a curse when it comes to finding work-personal life harmony. Women tend to overextend themselves, promise too much, try to deliver on everything, and feel guilty if they fail to do so.

Women aren't often as comfortable as men in drawing the line, setting boundaries, and working through one issue at a time. That kind of sequential thinking comes more naturally to a man. There is a solution though—a technique that can help women live in the moments we spoke of, with more focused attention.

CHUNKING TIME

At a recent gender-intelligence conference, I met Helen, CEO of a global oil company with its headquarters in the United States. She walked up to me with this big smile on her face and embraced me as if I were a long-lost friend saying, "I attended your keynote three years ago and remember your 'Chunk It' method. I've been practicing it ever since. It's not only improved my productivity at work, but it's also enhanced my personal life."

Generally speaking, women can't naturally do what men do— politely put up boundaries that limit the number of projects they'll get involved in. It doesn't necessarily limit their contribution though. It enables them to focus with singular intensity on a project right through to its completion—then onto the next. That's part of this "Chunking Time" idea.

"I can't partition my mind as easily," Helen continued. "Other activities will seep into my thoughts, and I have to tell myself intentionally that I will set my focus to one specific thing at a specific hour. I even enter events and commitments as appointments on my calendar. By portioning my time this way, I can focus on something or someone and it releases me from overthinking everything at once.

"I even practice 'Chunking Time' at home. When I'm with my husband or my daughter or son, it's not the quantity of time but the quality of time that I'm striving for—and that to my family means everything. My daughter would rather have five minutes of my undivided attention than an hour of interrupted thoughts and distractions.

I close off everything when I'm with her. I turn off the cell phone and delight in my time with her."

THE CHALLENGE FOR WOMEN

It seems a woman's brain is constantly working, and the higher her stress level, the more experiences and emotions she'll reflect on, find connections in, and attempt to resolve.

When at work, a woman will often be aware of the needs of every individual on her team, and she'll approach her personal life with the same presence and concentration. She'll focus on the needs of her family and friends, often putting her own needs last. There never seems to be enough time at work or even outside of work to attend to everything and everyone she feels deserves her attention. The challenge for women is not just finding harmony between work life and personal life, but finding harmony within and between each world—a coexistence of thoughts and activities while at work or at home.

THE CHALLENGE FOR MEN

For men, the challenge is often quite different. When a man is under stress, he'll typically develop tunnel vision and focus on one issue at a time. Generally speaking, that used to be the course of his workday, and at the end of the day, he would leave the workplace and its problems and issues behind with the thought, "Well, tomorrow is another day!" He would shift his attention to something else and forget about his work worries. This was how men separated work life from personal life: men would often come home from work, watch the news, read a paper, fix something simple around the house, or help with domestic chores.

But with Internet access and cloud computing, communication technologies and the structural aspects of work have changed, defining a new workplace in which men are more connected to their jobs

THE SCIENCE SIDE

One of the most important reasons why men and women react differently to stress is hormones, and three particular hormones play a crucial role: cortisol, oxytocin, and testosterone.

When cortisol rushes through a woman's bloodstream during a stressful situation, oxytocin is typically produced as its offsetting hormone. It's released from the brain, counteracts the production of cortisol, and promotes nurturing and relaxing emotions.[3]

While men also secrete the hormone oxytocin when they're stressed, it's often in far smaller amounts. Men will often react to their stress by either dealing with the situation or avoiding it if it proves too difficult to resolve. Women are more likely to face the issue. She'll tend to protect those close to her while creating and maintaining social networks to help reduce or eliminate the stressful situation. The instinctive actions of tending and befriending produce oxytocin in women, while the activities of fight-or-flight replenish testosterone in men.

While cortisol is an important and helpful trigger for the body's response to stress, it's important that the body's relaxation response be activated so the body's functions can return to normal following a stressful event. Unfortunately, in our current high-stress culture, the body's stress response is activated so often that the body doesn't always have a chance to return to normal, resulting in a state of chronic stress and anxiety.[4]

A woman's tendency is toward oxytocin-producing activities that lower her cortisol and reduce her stress, but when she's not able to engage in satisfying collaborative activities at work, or there's not enough time to attend to her nurturing relationships at home, then her stress and anxiety will increase beyond her ability to produce a relaxation response.

Studies have shown that women's cortisol levels at work tend to be twice as high as men's, and at home, their cortisol levels are four times higher than men's—a demonstration of the need for work-personal life harmony.[5]

"Relationship loss for women and performance failure for men are often the greatest stressors each sex experiences," according to psychologist Carl Pickhardt. "Because female self-esteem is often built around sufficiency of relationships and male self-esteem is often built around adequacy of performance, over-demand and insufficient" self-care tend to affect the mental and physical health of each gender differently.[6]

A woman is often at risk of letting other people's needs push her to her thresholds as she'll tend to subordinate her own needs until those of others are met. Men, on the other hand, often let challenge and competition push them to their limits. A man will tend to let his rival's efforts or his employer's agenda consume him, causing him to lose focus on himself and become preoccupied with attaining his objectives. He'll feel compelled to bring his work home.

---

beyond the boundaries of the traditional workday and workplace. Men can carry the office and all their unfinished projects and unresolved issues home, resulting in less time for a personal life.

HARMONY BEGINS WITH THE SELF

When we conduct workshops on work-personal life harmony, we ask questions of men and women to help them identify and express their life roles. Women will invariably identify all their roles and frame them as responsibilities to others, whether as a daughter, sister, girlfriend, wife, mother, or employee. One life role that's never in the lineup for women, regardless of the country, is that of "self."

It's very important to begin with one's own self, for the greatest value you can give to others is when you are whole and at your best. This is similar to flight attendants asking adults traveling with children to put their oxygen masks on first before helping children with theirs. You have to practice self-care before you can care for another, just as you have to love and value yourself first before you can give your love to another.

Men seldom seem to have a problem identifying themselves in their list of life roles and responsibilities. For example, a man will say, "I have a prior commitment" and not disclose all the details of what that prior commitment is. He may be taking his son to a football game! Men generally don't feel a need to justify why they're saying, "I need to leave," or "I'll look into it first thing in the morning," or "I can't get to that until next week."

Whether out of a sense of responsibility, other-oriented concern, or guilt, a woman often feels an obligation to explain herself and will begin listing all the details of why she needs to leave, or can't look into it until the morning, or has to put it off until next week.

A woman unknowingly loses respect in the male world because she often feels a need to justify her actions, while a man will tend to simply declare his intention.

"HI, I'M 98.5 PERCENT BILLABLE!"

Law firms have an interesting culture. Everything centers around billable hours. Partners with the most billable hours are the rainmakers and service the biggest and most prestigious clients.

In our work with a large law firm, we conducted workshops and one-on-one interviews with several partners to understand gender differences in working and succeeding in this culture. We learned that male attorneys consistently posted higher rates of billable hours than the women did. When asked why, the women lawyers all seemed to agree: "Our tendency is to over-scrutinize ourselves in our invoicing, wondering whether the hours we were charging could actually be considered billable."

The men had a different take on this. One lawyer, in a prideful tone and wanting to participate in the survey, introduced himself as, "Hi, I'm 98.5 percent billable, my name is Richard." Another male attorney went as far as saying, "If I'm even thinking about the client, I'm billing them!"

Two women attorneys who we interviewed started their own law firm in Europe several months later. An article about their business model attracted top women lawyers from different law firms in Europe and the United States who were tired of working long hours and constantly justifying their invoicing to the client.

"It's a painful and embarrassing thing to have to charge hours and minutes," they said. "We found another way—block pricing. Our board determines the time and resources required to handle a specific case, and we charge the client one cost for that particular service. The margins often worked to the client's favor, but client loyalty has increased and the number of clients expanded."

The billable hours model tends to keep clients at an arm's distance. With block pricing, clients feel they're being treated fairly. They know in advance what they'll be paying, with no surprise invoices. The women attorneys also discovered that they could devote as much time and attention to their clients' needs as necessary without having to watch the clock. Their focus shifted from measuring time to apportioning value.

"THEY'RE NEVER GOING TO BUY THIS!"

Miki, an Asian executive working in London, shares this with me: "I have these two women vice presidents reporting to me and they're both brilliant, but they want to leave the organization because they couldn't find enough work-personal life balance as vice presidents. Given the situations in each of their personal lives—one has pre-teens and the other now has an aging parent—they want to do something part time and out the ordinary, but they don't think it's going to be approved."

I ask her, "Have you figured out how you're going to present it to your boss?"

Miki responds, "Yes. I'm going to ask if the two women v-p's can job share. It's never been done but it would really help to retain both women."

I say, "You have to frame the request in such a way that a male will understand and find value in the arrangement. He already knows it will benefit the two women. He needs to see results and will be open to the most effective and efficient ways of getting there. Consider presenting it as an innovative idea not only to retain top talent, but to create an even greater services resource to the client and a cost efficiency for the company."

Weeks later, Miki calls me to share that her reframing the job-sharing idea as an improvement in performance won the two women their part-time vice presidencies. "I would never have thought to frame it as you had. I would have walked in asking for his help in accommodating these two women instead of positioning it as a success story. It's now become a new model for retaining and attracting key talent, combining forces to be even more effective for the client, and paying less money in salary. Men are even showing interest."

"HOW CAN I HAVE IT ALL IF SHE CAN'T?"

Before delivering my keynote address for a rather large investment bank, I was invited into the company's online chat room where women ages 25 to 35 were blogging—"You can't have a life and a career. Read what that woman executive is saying in her article, *You Can't Have It All.*"

The author was admitting, to younger and older women alike, that it's impossible to pursue a career and have a life because women do so much more than men and have so much less in work-personal life balance. So the author shared how she quit because she couldn't have the career she wanted and the personal life she desired at the same time. Another woman blogging her response sums it up this way: "How can I have it all if she can't?"

She *can* have it all. She just doesn't need to do it all!

Work and personal will always be competing lives for women try-ing to find balance instead of congruity.

A woman *can* be as ambitious as she wants to be, build a successful career that she can be proud of, *and* have a personal life that brings her joy and satisfaction—regardless of whether she's single or married, and with or without children or others to care for.

"She can have it all, but she doesn't need to do it all" is a strong mes-sage we are imparting to women in this chapter—a valuable insight to a younger generation in the process of planning or building their careers.

A woman will never "have it all" if she continually puts others first, never says "no" or "later," and never self-cares—all out of a sense of guilt. Guilt increases stress, and when a woman's stress levels increase, the never-ending to-do list for others surfaces. Women tend to place themselves at the bottom of that list.

Why go out for cocktails after work, or stay up all night when traveling with associates? Men find no difficulty or sense of guilt when they say, "I'm going to call it an evening. You guys have fun." A man typically doesn't mean anything personal by it, and he doesn't expect the other guys to be upset if he were to say, "See you later!"

As young girls, many women are often conditioned to believe that they're being selfish when they think of themselves and not others. Building relationships requires empathy, the giving of one's time and attention, then receiving similar concern in return. In reality, practicing self-care tends to reduce a woman's stress and allows her to think more fully. It gives her the feeling that she's not alone and that she's supported and connected, making her more valuable to others in the long run.

THE PERSONAL SIDE OF LIFE

Many believe that quality time with children mostly occurs when there is quantity of time. The thinking is, "The more time I have, the more opportunity for there to be quality time." Many parents have quantity time, but they're not connecting often enough and in memorable ways with their children. Showing up, or always being there, or making every game doesn't necessarily result in quality time.

There was a time when families primarily lived on farms, and children worked closely with their parents and were able to absorb their parents' values and ethics. They watched how their mom and dad dealt with situations and reacted to problems. They even noticed how mom and dad reacted to each other—how mom showed support and dad showed affection. Children were in close proximity to their parents most every day of their earlier, developmental years, right up through adolescence.

Today, it's the values of teachers and other children at school that our children are absorbing. Quite often, it's the schoolyard bully who has the strongest effect on our children as they seek his or her approval.

Today, with both parents working, we have to adapt by developing better communication skills. Adults have to learn how to *listen* to their children. Engaging children in conversation helps them feel safe and motivated to tell you about their day. We can still instill our values in our children by simply listening as they talk and by reinforcing special times created together.

Ask adults what they remember most about childhood and they'll recall events that centered around a family tradition or ritual. The family meal, a holiday gathering, or even a nightly bedtime routine of looking for objects in an *I Spy* book are all memorable events in a child's mind.

Children do far better in households where ritual is established and preserved, even in the face of disruptive problems such as divorce or alcoholism. When family members are upset with each other, daily rituals can pull them back together and provide the setting for working out problems.

Family rituals enhance a child's identity, provide stability and calm during times of stress, and connect generations in a perpetual bond—daughters with mother with grandmother. Routine establishes so many aspects of healthy living, good habits, and good behavior that even the slightest structure is valuable to a child, creating positive memories and a feeling of harmony.

EPILOGUE

SMART WOMEN AND MEN, WORKING AND WINNING TOGETHER

WHEN WE BEGAN PURSUING OUR INDIVIDUAL PRACTICES 30 years ago, we were steadfast in our desire to help women and men find greater understanding and success in their working lives, and to help them as partners and parents find greater understanding, trust, and meaning in their personal lives.

Although we had set upon our own separate paths, we were united in the belief that gender intelligence—understanding, appreciating, and valuing gender differences—would improve the professional and personal happiness of men and women all over the world.

When we reflect back to the first time we met in 2009, we knew that our coming together and writing this book was emblematic of women's and men's desire not only to understand and be understood in the workplace and at home, but to find greater harmony between their work life and personal life—in other words, to have these lives coexist and not compete. We saw this ongoing challenge requiring even greater understanding and cooperation between women and men, a consideration for each other that can only come from gender intelligence.

As we look forward, we can't help but imagine what the world would be like if it were filled with men and women—at all levels of leadership and in all walks of life—possessing such gender intelligence. What if we understood, appreciated, and valued each other well enough and genuinely enough to the point where men could speak for women and women could speak for men?

Imagine the spirit of collaboration, creativity, and productivity that would exist in businesses throughout the world. The engagement of highly educated yet underutilized women would have such an amazing economic impact, particularly in countries facing talent shortages expressly because their traditional cultures undervalue women and relegate them to conventional roles.

Imagine couples living in fulfilling relationships and finding greater love through an enhanced understanding and appreciation for each other. Imagine gender-intelligent mothers and fathers becoming better parents to their daughters and sons, helping raise cooperative, confident, and compassionate children, and giving them the freedom and direction to express their authentic selves.

Imagine governments working together to find pathways to peace and prosperity through enhanced dialogue. Imagine country leaders working to end forever the maiming and killing of their young girls and the suppression of their women.

It is not out of our reach or idealistic to think that women and men, working together, can make our world a better place. This is what we characterize as gender intelligence—men and women seeing the world through each other's eyes and valuing each other's line of sight.

STRENGTH IN DIFFERENCE

Great minds don't always think alike; great minds often think differently. Difference thinking often makes all the difference in the world!

Men's and women's brains have tremendous strength in the workplace and are even stronger when brought together. The old adage "*the whole is greater than the sum of its parts*" could not be truer when applied to men and women coming together to solve problems, make decisions, and lead. We see difference thinking as a valuable dynamic companies and other organizations will continue to discover in our increasingly diverse workplace and global marketplace.

Many of the studies that we've presented in our book point to the fact that teams containing a better balance of women to men achieve higher results in innovation and effectiveness. These behavioral studies show that in gender-blended groups in which everyone feels comfortable and all opinions are heard, teams are more likely to challenge established norms and get the best ideas on the table.

This is not because men and women are so basically different or that women are more clever, more empathetic, or better than men. It is because women and men bring different viewpoints and experiences to the table and, as a result, add a richer collection of perspectives and values to the decision-making process. Where men's management style is more transactional, risk-accepting, and solutions-driven, women's management style is characterized as more contextual and relationship-based, encouraging and empowering greater discussion and ideation.

Women's values in unity with men's are improving the quality of life for employees by bringing personal fulfillment into the workplace, creating an even greater bottom line because everyone is included and contributing in his or her own authentic way. The zero-sum way of thinking "I win, you lose" is being replaced by an inclusive "we win" outlook. This is one of the greatest shifts occurring in corporations today.

Another major shift is the definition and practice of inclusive leadership. Many companies today are still operating on a hero model of leadership, believing that if an organization has the one right person in place, then all will be well. Corporations that operate this way and do not involve all internal stakeholders will end up paying dearly in the years to come.

It's very difficult for companies to escape the mindset of the twentieth century and the quest for the hero leader. But as we venture further into the twenty-first century, the focus of senior management will necessarily turn away from leaders intent on position and power to those who lead by encouraging ideas, from leaders who act as the iconic, external voice of the company to leaders who embody the uniting, enabling voice within the company and behind all its talent.

Multinational companies today face business opportunities and challenges that are deeply complex and interconnected. These organizations are comprised of thousands of employees in dozens of countries with varying cultural and political differences, and with variations in their work ethic, reporting structures, and goals. No one leader can possibly hold all the answers to all the problems, challenges, and opportunities facing such vast organizations.

The hierarchal, heroic approach to leadership in the past will most likely yield to an ensemble leadership style over the next decade and become the dominant trait of the global leader in the years to come. The responsibilities that were once the domain of one leader will disperse to other stewards in the enterprise and in other regions of the world. No longer the single source of knowledge, wisdom, and decision, the twenty-first-century leader will become an integrator of knowledge. The leader of the future will not be a singularly powerful individual prone to making decisions in isolation. He or she will be a team player, willing to collaborate and obsessed with enabling value through others—traits very much like those that women leaders bring to the table.

When we meld the dynamic, eclectic, collaborative attitudes and behaviors of women with the systematic, focused, results-oriented thoughts and actions of men, we achieve something neither gender could ever hope to realize on its own. And from that natural complement, all sorts of amazing things can and will happen!

We envision a day when our gender blind spots will become a thing of the past and a book of this nature will no longer be required. We envision a day when gender-intelligent men and women will seek out each other's authentic nature and work and live together in a naturally occurring and openly inviting way. This is a goal worth attaining—a world deserving of all men and women, in partnership and unity.

IF YOU LIKED WHAT YOU'VE READ AND WANT TO GROW IN YOUR GENDER INTELLIGENCE

Arrange for keynotes or seminars with Barbara Annis and John Gray.

Schedule Gender Intelligence Workshops for your company or organization. The "aha" moments will astound you!

Take The Global Gender Intelligence Assessment©, a valuable online self-assessment tool designed to help you better understand gender, become more inclusive, and improve your effectiveness in the workplace.

Learn more about the *Work with Me* webinar series, helping individuals and teams uncover their blind spots and discover greater success in their work lives and personal lives!

Visit:
http://www.baainc.com
http://www.marsvenus.com

ABOUT THE AUTHORS

Barbara Annis is the world-renowned expert on Gender Intelligence® and inclusive leadership, advocating the value and practice of Gender Intelligence in over 60 Fortune 500 companies, 10 governments, and numerous organizations across the globe. Her insights and achievements have pioneered a transformational shift in cultural attitudes on the importance of gender unity to personal and organizational success. Her book, *Same Words, Different Language* is considered a seminal contribution to the new conversation between men and women at work. She serves as Chair Emeritus of the Women's Leadership Board at the Harvard Kennedy School and was recently conferred the International Alliance for Women, Lifetime Achievement Award.

John Gray, Ph.D., is the leading relationship expert in the world and bestselling relationship author of all time. His book, *Men Are from Mars, Women Are from Venus,* is ranked by *USA Today* as one of the top 10 most influential books over the last 25 years. His 17 books have been published in 50 different languages, and he is a popular keynote speaker for international organizations and Fortune 500 companies. He is the founder of Mars Venus Coaching, and has personally trained over 500 coaches in 27 countries to bridge the gender gap in business through gender-smart leadership, sales, and team-building training programs.

NOTES

CHAPTER 1: ARE WE REALLY THE SAME?

1. U.S. Equal Employment Opportunity Commission, Sexual Harassment Charges, EEOC & FEPAs Combined: FY 1997-FY 2011.
2. Gender Surveys, Barbara Annis & Associates, 2005–2012.
3. Grant Thornton International Business Report, 2010.
4. Nicholas Kristof and Sheryl WuDunn, *Half the Sky: Turning Oppression into Opportunity for Women Worldwide* (New York: Knopf, 2009).
5. "Female Leadership, A Competitive Edge for the Future," McKinsey & Company, 2009.
6. "The Strengths Revolution," Gallop Management Journal, January 22, 2001.
7. "Current Population Reports: Series P-20," No. 373, Table 4.
8. "Women in Senior Management," Goldman Sachs, 2010.
9. "For First Time, More Women than Men Earn PhD," *USA Today*, September 14, 2010, http://usatoday30.usatoday.com/news/education/2010-09-15-women phd14_st_N.htm.
10. "Collective Intelligence: Number of Women in Group Lead to Effectiveness in Solving Difficult Problems," *ScienceDaily*, October 2, 2010, http://www.sciencedaily.com/releases/2010/09/100930143339.htm.

CHAPTER 2: DO WOMEN WANT MEN TO CHANGE?

1. Gender Surveys, Barbara Annis & Associates, 2005–2012.
2. Stephan Hamann, "Sex Differences in the Responses of the Human Amygdala," *The Neuroscientist* 11:4 (2005), 288-293.
3. Louann Brizendine, *The Female Brain* (New York: Three Rivers Press, Crown Publishing 2007), http://rnawrocki.com/pdfs/Louann%20Brizendine%20-%20 The%20Female%20Brain.pdf.
4. Hamann, "Sex Differences in the Responses of the Human Amygdala."
5. Anne Moir and David Jessel, *Brain Sex: The Real Differences between Men and Women* (New York: Dell Publishing, 1992), pp. 39-49.

CHAPTER 3: DO MEN APPRECIATE WOMEN?

1. Gender Surveys, Barbara Annis & Associates, 2005–2012.
2. Towers Perrin Global Workforce Study, 2007–2008.
3. Gender Surveys, Barbara Annis & Associates, 2005–2012.

4. "Women-Owned Businesses in the 21st Century," U.S. Department of Commerce, October 2010.
5. M. E. Frederikse, A. Lu, E. Aylward, P. Barta, G. Pearlson, "Sex Differences In the Inferior Parietal Lobule," 1999, http://cercor.oxfordjournals.org/content/9/8/896 .long.
6. "Male vs. Female, The Brain Differences," Columbia University, http://www.colum bia.edu/itc/anthropology/v1007/jakabovics/mf2.html.

CHAPTER 4: ARE WOMEN BEING EXCLUDED?

1. Gender Surveys, Barbara Annis & Associates, 2005–2012.
2. "US Women Lawyers Likely to Leave Employers Three Years Earlier Than Men," HRM Guide Human Resources, January 2001, http://www.hrmguide.net/usa /women_lawyers.htm.
3. Kathleen M. Mahoney, "He Said/She Said: Jurors' Perceptions of Women Advocates," *The Woman Advocate*, American Bar Association Section of Litigation, 1999, 4-6, http://womenaslawyers.wordpress.com/.
4. Ibid.
5. *Women in the World's Legal Professions*, ed. Ulrike Schultz and Gisela Shaw (Oxford, UK: Hart Publishing, 2003), 41-42.
6. Shelley E. Taylor, Laura Cousino Klein, Brian P. Lewis, Tara L. Gruenewald, Regan A. R. Gurung, and John A. Updegraff, "Biobehavioral Responses to Stress in Females: Tend-and-Befriend, Not Fight-or-Flight," *Psychological Review*, July 2000, 107:3, 411-429.
7. Michael G. Conner, "Understanding the Difference Between Men and Women," http://www.oregoncounseling.org/ArticlesPapers/Documents/DifferencesMen Women.htm.
8. Taylor et al., "Biobehavioral Responses to Stress in Females: Tend-and-Befriend, Not Fight-or-Flight."

CHAPTER 5: DO MEN HAVE TO WALK ON EGGSHELLS WITH WOMEN?

1. Gender Surveys, Barbara Annis & Associates, 2005–2012.
2. U.S. Equal Employment Opportunity Commission, Sexual Harassment Charges, EEOC & FEPAs Combined: FY1997-FY2011.
3. Jean Hollands, *Same Game, Different Rules: How to Avoid Being a Bully Broad, Ice Queen, or Ms. Understood* (New York: McGraw-Hill, 2002), xxiii.
4. "The Role of Emotion in Memory," http://www.memory-key.com/memory /emotion.
5. "Neuroscientists Find that Men and Women Respond Differently to Stress," *Science Daily*, April 1, 2008, http://www.sciencedaily.com/videos/2008/0403-men_are _from_mars.htm
6. Larry Cahill, "His Brain, Her Brain," *Scientific American*, May 2005, 46-47.
7. Grant Thornton International Business Report, 2012, http://www.gti.org/files /ibr2012%20-%20women%20in%20senior%20management%20master.pdf, 3.

CHAPTER 6: DO WOMEN ASK TOO MANY QUESTIONS?

1. Gender Surveys, Barbara Annis & Associates, 2005–2012.

2. Louann Brizendine, *The Female Brain* (New York: Three Rivers Press, Crown Publishing, 2007), http://rnawrocki.com/pdfs/Louann%20Brizendine%20-%20The%20Female%20Brain.pdf.

3. Michael Gurian and Kathy Stevens, "With Boys and Girls in Mind," *Educational Leadership,* Nov. 2004, http://www.ascd.org/publications/educational-leadership/nov04/vo162/num03/with-boys-and-girls-in-mind.aspx.

4. Helen Fisher, "The Natural Leadership Talents of Women," in *Enlightened Power: How Women Are Transforming the Practice of Leadership,* eds. Linda Coughlin, Ellen Wingard, Keith Hollihan, eds. (San Francisco, CA: Jossey Bass, 2005), ch.8, http://www.helenfisher.com/downloads/articles/07leadership.pdf.

5. "More Female Bankers Could Have Prevented the Financial Crisis," *The Grindstone,* Jan. 2012, http://thegrindstone.com/office-politics/analysts-say-having-more-female-bankers-could-have-prevented-the-financial-crisis-181/.

CHAPTER 7: DO MEN LISTEN?

1. Gender Surveys, Barbara Annis & Associates, 2005–2012.

2. "Intelligence in Men and Women Is a Gray and White Matter," *Science Daily,* January 20, 2005, http://www.sciencedaily.com/releases/2005/01/050121100142.htm; Molly Edmonds, "Differences in Male and Female Brain Structure," *Discovery Fitness & Health,* http://health.howstuffworks.com/human-body/systems/nervous-system/men-women-different-brains1.htm.

3. "Intelligence in Men and Women Is a Gray and White Matter," *Science Daily,* January 20, 2005, http://www.sciencedaily.com/releases/2005/01/050121100142.htm.

4. Tori DeAngelis, "The Two Faces of Oxytocin," American Psychological Association, Feb 2008, 39:2, http://www.apa.org/monitor/feb08/oxytocin.aspx.

CHAPTER 8: ARE WOMEN TOO EMOTIONAL?

1. Gender Surveys, Barbara Annis & Associates, 2005–2012.

2. Stephan Hamann, "Sex Differences in the Responses of the Human Amygdala," *The Neuroscientist* 11:4 (2005), 288-293.

CHAPTER 9: ARE MEN INSENSITIVE?

1. Gender Surveys, Barbara Annis & Associates, 2005–2012.

2. "Collective Intelligence: Number of Women in Group Linked to Effectiveness in Solving Difficult Problems," *ScienceDaily,* October 2010, http://www.sciencedaily.com/releases/2010/09/100930143339.htm.

3. Emily Deans, "Dopamine, the Left Brain, Women, and Men," *Psychology Today,* May 17, 2011, http://www.psychologytoday.com/blog/evolutionary-psychiatry/201105/dopamine-the-left-brain-women-and-men.

4. Schulte-Ruther, Markowitsch, Shah, Fink, and Picfke, "Gender Differences in Brain Networks Supporting Empathy," Institute of Neuroscience and Biophysics, April 2008, p. 1, http://perso.ens-lyon.fr/annececile.boulay/UE%20biblio/pdf/7.5.Schulte-Ruther.NeuroImage08.pdf.

5. Louann Brizendine, *The Female Brain* (New York: Three Rivers Press, Crown Publishing 2007), p. TK, http://rnawrocki.com/pdfs/Louann%20Bhrizendine%20-%20The%20Female%20Brain.pdf.

CHAPTER 10: BUILDING TRUST WITH WOMEN, INCREASING CREDIBILITY WITH MEN

1. Gender Surveys, Barbara Annis & Associates, 2005–2012.
2. Susan Kuchinskas, *The Chemistry of Connection: How the Oxytocin Response Can Help You Find Trust, Intimacy, and Love* (Oakland, CA: New Harbinger Publications, 2009), pp. 6-9.
3. Paul J. Zak, "The Neurobiology of Trust," *Scientific American,* June 2008, http://www.templeton.org/pdfs/press_releases/Paul%20Zak.Neurobiology%20of%20Trust.pdf.
4. Louann Brizendine, "The Female Brain," (New York: Three Rivers Press, 2007) p 95, http://www.drlumd.com/wp-content/uploads/2011/12/The-Female-Brain.pdf.

CHAPTER 11: BRIDGING OUR DIFFERENT VALUES

1. Gender Surveys, Barbara Annis & Associates, 2005–2012.
2. History from IKEA home page at http://www.ikea.com/ms/en_US/about_ikea/the_ikea_way/history/index.html.
3. Audrey Nelson, "Can Men Play the Negotiation Game Better than Women?" *Psychology Today,* June 19, 2011, http://www.psychologytoday.com/blog/he-speaks-she-speaks/201106/can-men-play-the-negotiation-game-better-women.
4. M. E. Frederikse, A. Lu, E. Aylward, P. Barta, G. Pearlson "Sex Differences In the Inferior Parietal Lobule," 1999, http://cercor.oxfordjournals.org/content/9/8/896.long.
5. "Male vs. Female, The Brain Differences," Columbia University, http://www.columbia.edu/itc/anthropology/v1007/jakabovics/mf2.html.
6. "Sex Differences In the Inferior Parietal Lobule," M. E. Frederikse, A. Lu, E. Aylward, P. Barta, G. Pearlson (1999), http://cercor.oxfordjournals.org/content/9/8/896.long.
7. "When Does Gender Matter in Negotiation?" Hannah Riley and Kathleen L. McGinn, Working paper, September 2002, 18, web.hks.harvard.edu/publications/getFile.aspx?Id=51.
8. "Female Leadership, A Competitive Edge for the Future," McKinsey & Company, 2009.

CHAPTER 12: ACHIEVING WORK-PERSONAL LIFE HARMONY

1. Employment Characteristics of Families Summary, April 2012, http://www.bls.gov/news.release/famee.nr0.htm.
2. Gender Surveys, Barbara Annis & Associates, 2005–2012.
3. "Why Men and Women Handle Stress Differently," reviewed by Brunilda Nazario, MD, http://women.webmd.com/features/stress-women-men-cope.
4. Ibid.
5. "The Handbook of Stress Science: Biology, Psychology, and Health," ed. Richard Contrada, Andrew Baum (New York: Springer Publishing, 2010), pp. 536-539.
6. Carl Pickhardt, quoted in WebMD feature, "Why Men and Women Handle Stress Differently," http://women.webmd.com/features/stress-women-men-cope.

INDEX